CREATIVE DANCE IN THE SECONDARY SCHOOL

CREATIVE DANCE IN THE SECONDARY SCHOOL

by

Joan Russell

Principal Lecturer in Dance
Worcester College of Education

MACDONALD & EVANS LTD.

8 John Street, London WC1N 2HY

1969

First Published October, 1969
Reprinted March, 1971
Reprinted September, 1972

©

MACDONALD & EVANS LTD
1969

S.B.N.: 7121 0320 1

Printed in Great Britain by
UNWIN BROTHERS LIMITED
WOKING AND LONDON

Preface

Creative Dance in the Secondary School is a companion to *Creative Dance in the Primary School* and follows a similar format. It presents a case for the inclusion of dance and dance drama in both the middle and the secondary school, stressing the importance of the provision of opportunities for creative activity as a balance to the more academic side of the curriculum. The introduction of dance into the secondary school and the teacher's task in teaching the subject are both discussed in separate chapters. The analysis in Chapter 4 includes some material first published, in a chapter similarly entitled, in *Creative Dance in the Primary School*, but with additional material added as appropriate to the secondary school. The same applies to some of the material included in the syllabus for Years 1 and 2. This repetition of material is included in order to present a full picture for secondary teachers and to avoid unnecessary reference to another publication.

The core of the book is a suggested syllabus given year by year and based on the sixteen basic movement themes as set out by Laban in *Modern Educational Dance*. Preparation for this section has been carried out in an intensive programme over the last three years. After a year of observation of all age groups in a secondary school selected for the main experimental work, a proposed syllabus was drawn up in consultation with a group of practising teachers. This was tried out in the next two years in the school and forms the basis of the material suggested here. Further discussions with the original group of teachers and with others have taken place, as have visits to other schools to look at the work in dance. No differentiation of material has been suggested for boys since it is the author's contention that a balanced choice of themes, with choice within themes, gives scope for a variety of response. In the school at which the main work was carried out, mixed classes have been taken for dance in the first and second C streams in the last two years. Hence photographs of boys are included. The only significant fact to record in this connection is the children's preference to work in groups of similar sex. This section includes photographs of pupils in the first four years of the secondary school.

The photographs have been selected from a large number taken during

5

class work with pupils from the first to the fourth year in Nunnery Wood Secondary School, Worcester. In the case of those of *Theseus* and the *Gloria* the dances had already been worked out by the girls. All the other photographs show the pupils working on tasks given as part of a normal lesson. They were in no way rehearsed, although the material was familiar. The purpose of including these illustrations is to record the children's response to material given in the syllabus suggested in Chapters 5 to 9. The captions accompanying the plates draw attention to the children's interpretation of the tasks set, in terms of action, movement quality and relationship and aim to aid the teacher's observation.

J. R.

August 1969

Acknowledgments

IT would have been impossible to carry out such an intensive programme of observation, and so bring authenticity to the syllabus suggested here, without the ready co-operation of Mr. A. J. Sinclair, headmaster of Nunnery Wood Secondary School, and Miss Brenda Jones, the teacher in charge of the dance at the school. I should like to record my grateful thanks to them both for their generous help and encouragement. I am also indebted to Miss J. R. F. Wilks, the headmistress of King Edward VI High School for Girls, Birmingham, to Mrs. V. N. Wilkinson, headmistress of Crossgate County Secondary Girls' School, Leeds, to Miss P. Blumer, headmistress of Bridgnorth Secondary Girls' School and Mr. T. D. J. Potter, headmaster of Samuel Southall Secondary School, Worcester, for allowing me to visit their schools to look at the work in dance. My thanks are due to the following who so kindly discussed their work with me on several occasions: Mrs. M. Pain, Mrs. J. Whalley, Miss P. Smith, Miss S. Haigh and Miss J. Jeffries. I am also grateful to Miss Brenda Jones, who read the manuscript and suggested valuable emendations, as well as assisting me in reading the proofs.

My thanks are due to the following for permission to quote extracts from their publications: Harvard University Press for extracts from *The Creative Arts in American Education* by Munro and *On Knowing—essays for the left hand* by Prof. Bruner; Dance Horizons for the extract from *Letters on Dancing and Ballet* by Noverre, translated by Cyril W. Beaumont; the Hutchinson Publishing Group for the extracts from *Taken Care Of* by Edith Sitwell; Ted Shawn for the extract from *Every Little Movement*; Rene Cutforth for the extract from "The Swedes don't have the answer" published by the *Radio Times*, and *The Daily Telegraph Colour Supplement* for the extract from "The Pueblo Tribes" by John Masters. My grateful thanks are due to the photographer, Mr. Geoffrey Hopcraft, for his understanding and skill, and to Mrs. Doris Wenham for help in preparing the index.

J.R.

Contents

Chapter

Preface 5

Acknowledgments. 7

1. Dance, the primary art 11

2. The place of dance in the middle school . . 19

3. Introducing dance in the secondary school . . 24

4. Thinking in terms of movement: an analysis . . 33

5. First Year Secondary, aged 11–12 47

6. Second Year Secondary, aged 12–13 . . . 54

7. Third Year Secondary, aged 13–14 60

8. Fourth Year Secondary, aged 14–15 . . . 70

9. Fifth to Seventh Year Secondary, aged 15–18 . 80

10. The teacher's task 86

Bibliography 99

Index 101

CHAPTER 1

Dance, the primary art

HISTORY reveals that dance has had many faces and has served many needs through the ages, whether of magical, ritualistic, religious, sociological or educational significance. Dance has been a spontaneous expression of feeling, it has been carefully composed, it has been enjoyed as a communal activity, it has been performed as a spectacle.

In education various forms of dance have been used ranging from the primitive war and hunting dances which inculcated some of the actions employed in such activities, to the minuet and gavotte, which laid stress on deportment, to the revived Maypole dances, which looked with nostalgia to a rural England. In recent years a number of different forms have been introduced into the secondary school programme. The Greek Dance of the 1930s was followed by the English Country Dance, European National Dance Styles and Central European Dance, a forerunner of Modern Educational Dance, the essential philosophy of which is embodied in the name. It is not only, of course, that this type of dance is suitable for teaching in schools. Rather, it is that the whole approach sets out to give such opportunities to those engaged in it that the experience gained thereby provides scope for their potentialities and thus educates and recreates them. When introducing this approach in his book *Modern Educational Dance* Laban wrote:

"A third task is the fostering of artistic expression in the medium of the primary art of movement. Here two quite distinct aims will have to be pursued. One is to aid the creative expression of children by producing dances adequate to their gifts and to the stage of their development. The other is to foster the capacity for taking part in the higher unit of communal dances produced by the teacher.

A further task can be seen in the awakening of a broad outlook on human activities through the observation of the flow of movement used in them."

and

"It should be mentioned finally that the new dance technique endeavours to integrate intellectual knowledge with creative ability, an aim which is of paramount importance in any form of education."

In the primary school our aim is to preserve the child's spontaneity and liveliness, to foster his creative ability and to involve him in activities which serve an integrating function. In the secondary school the need remains the same. Indeed one can go further and say that the need to fulfil such educational aims is greater. The primary school child does at least tend to be regarded as a whole being. He frequently takes part in project work where his abilities in mathematics, science, art and craft, drama, dance and written work may be harnessed in connection with a centre of interest. In this way are demonstrated not only the interrelationship of so-called subjects but, more important, the relationship between his several faculties of mind and body. In secondary education the stress is all too often on the academic development.

Munro's comments on American education in the arts, made in the Inglis Lecture in 1960, apply equally to our own system today. He said:

"The value of the arts in general education is now widely recognised, much more so than fifty years ago. But in practice they are often pushed aside by other pressures. Our education has been on the whole too exclusively verbal, intellectual and practical. For an adequately balanced, diversified program in general education, it needs more effort to develop the student's powers of sense perception, imagination, emotional sensitivity, and bodily control in the techniques of art."

It seems vital that older children, and adolescents in particular, should have scope for their physical, intuitive and emotional, as well as their intellectual, faculties. This they can do only if artistic activities are included in the curriculum. Here dance has a major part to play since participation in this aspect of the primary art of movement gives scope to foster artistic expression. It is perhaps important to enlarge upon this view of the art of movement as the "primary" art. The inference here is not that the art of movement is more important than other arts, although it is very important as a creative activity. The first significant fact to support this idea of dance as the primary art is its emergence so early in the history of man. Dancing may well be the oldest of the arts since it needs no instrument other than the dancer's body. The accompaniment which came from stamping feet, clapping hands and voice sounds supplied the rhythm.

It is difficult to produce evidence of an activity as transitory as dance. Nevertheless, the prehistoric cave paintings show that dance was at least contemporaneous with painting. Evidence of this is seen in such cave paintings as that of the dancing sorcerer wearing the mask of a deer, found in a cave near Ariège in France, said to be the first known picture of a supernatural dance. Such early ritual dances were developed from man's first strivings for communication with the gods and his desire for shared communication with his fellows. In primitive communities dance was, and still is, vital to his well-being. It is interesting to note that the visual arts served the ritual with the reproduction of deities, masks, ritual objects, totems and fetishes.

Not only do paintings, friezes, decorations on cups and urns testify to the antiquity of the art of dance but also there is much supporting evidence to be found in the written word:

"Thus in olden times did the Cretan women dance to the tune of music, with tender feet, around the charming altar, treading the soft flowers of the lawn."

Sappho of Lesbos

"And they followed, singing and dancing with fervour and stamped the ground in unison. And now they danced fast in a circle like a wheel . . . and now they separated into two ranks, advancing towards each other. And the crowd pressed around them charmed."

Homer—*The Iliad*, XVIII

"This dance shows suppleness and rectitude and excellence of body and soul, which their bearing and their acts suggest."

Plato—*Laws*, "The Pyrrhic"

13

Dance is not only to be seen as an interesting phenomenon of ancient cultures. Nor is it only to be seen performed by groups in under-developed countries as a spectacle for the tourist. Dance can still be found as a living force in the lives of some people today. Evidence of the importance of dance to the Indians of New Mexico has been given in an article by John Masters.* He writes of the Spring Corn Dance performed on May 1st, 1968, at San Felipe:

"Four o'clock, five o'clock. The Anglos have been drifting off since noon, guilty that they do not have the patience to stay to the end, uncomfortable because they do not understand the dance, and uneasily aware that their world lost something valuable when everyone stopped dancing round the maypole. When, now, do we get together to express joy or one-ness? At all our great occasions—football matches, elections, race meetings—we express only our freedom of choice, our individuality. Perhaps the Indian is surer of those things than we are.

I look carefully at the old man with the typoni. His arms must ache from holding the great pole all day against the relentless wind, and the strain of waving it about, like a wand. He, too, is a figure from the remote pre-history of a remote continent, but the human being inside those gaudy vestments could be Nawee Sintza, Zuni. Sintza is a jeweller, silversmith and lapidary; and he also programmes, operates, and maintains an automatic wave soldering machine for electronic wire harness assemblies. He learned those skills at a speed which staggered the Anglo firm that brought its factory to Zuni to help provide jobs for his people.

And the dancing girl with the short hair, paired by chance with a man for the rites of the dance, she might be an ignorant village lass, or she might be Viola Nieto, who works in the same factory as Nawee Sintza and is a niece of the great jeweller Dan Simplicio. Any of these women (sweating, intent, black-clothed, bejewelled, priestly, hands waving the spruce boughs) might be a manicurist, telephone girl, punch-card operator, receptionist.

I had learned that understanding of the pueblos does not come through explanations, but through the eyes, the ears, and the pores of the skin. It is not a cerebral but a visceral thing, and it is best expressed by this most

* *Daily Telegraph Colour Supplement.*

14

distinctive feature of pueblo life—their great ceremonial dances, such as at Santo Domingo on August 1, Tesuque on November 12, and this Spring Corn Dance that we are watching, at San Felipe every May 1.

Typical to the rest of pueblo thought, these dances are not susceptible of explanation in logical terms. Like Mount Everest, they are. Ask an Indian their purpose, and to get rid of the question he will answer: 'To pray for rain . . . or crops . . . or grace.' But in fact to him the question is unanswerable.

If we can say anything, we can say only that the dances are a mystical celebration of the unity of all nature, which is the foundation of the pueblo Indians' faith. To him religion is not outside but inside and it is universal.

The music and the chanting stopped abruptly, and the whole kiva group, 300 strong, filed past, not looking at any of us, Anglo or Indian. No one not of the dance existed. The dancers were one with the earth they danced on and the air that gave them energy. They flung themselves down to rest—mystics, artists, mothers, craftsmen, farmers, politicians, typists, lawyers, mechanics, all one—Corn Dancers.

Obviously, nothing had been solved and, obviously, everything had."

More important, however, than the historical significance of dance is the fact that this art form is rooted in the first means of expression and communication of the human being. Before birth the movement of the unborn child can be felt and indeed the Swedish photographer Lennart Nilsson has photographed a live embryo using original equipment designed for him by Werner Donner. He described his excitement as he saw a hand appear and the foetus slowly sucking its thumb. From the moment of birth the baby moves with increasing range and ability to express needs and feelings and through his movement reveals his personality.

In human beings we observe two strivings. Laban referred to them as "doing" and "dancing." Allport, writing of expressive behaviour in his book *Pattern and Growth in Personality* (1961), uses the terms "coping" and "expressive behaviour." He maintains that every action betrays both a coping and an expressive aspect—coping is concerned with WHAT we are doing and expression with HOW—but the proportion of these varies widely.

It is interesting to recall that primitive man relied very much on the results of his own movement in working actions (coping) and he extended these movements in a rhythmical way to create working dances (expressive behaviour).

Allport refers to the work of the German psychologist, Ludvig Klages, who made a sharp distinction in his "stratification theory" between the upper overlaid layer *Geist* (mind, intellect, adaptive performance) which produces "coping" and the *Seele* (the soul, the diffuse elemental surge of life) which is concerned with expression. The former acts as a restrainer, and, he suggests, sometimes as a destroyer even, of the basic rhythms that are carriers of vital expression. One wonders if there might be some verification for this idea when considering the state of many highly mechanised modern societies. Writing about his film *One Pair of Eyes*,* Rene Cutforth has these relevant things to say:

> "It is assumed in Sweden that life consists of changing the environment, and always in the direction of mechanical perfection . . .
>
> The Swedes have now reached the stage when the mechanical details are all but perfect, society is a precision mechanism of well-oiled cogs. Unfortunately, quite a large number of people don't seem to want to function in it. The drunk, the drug addict, the tramp, the delinquent have all been swept up into care of the most radical and rational kind— prisons are like holiday camps—but this sociologists' dream turns out to be a human nightmare. A gigantic 'So what?' writes itself up in the collective mind."

As educationists we are familiar with the fact that personality and mood are shown in expressive behaviour, and that this is strongly manifest in the child, while with growing maturity and the exercise of control, expression becomes confined to limited regions of the body and a personal style is developed. For those who have been concerned to study human movement, accounts of investigations into this aspect of behaviour during the last two hundred years are of interest. Noverre is said to have sent his pupils into the streets and market-places to observe movement. In one of his letters on dancing he wrote of workmen:

* Article in *Radio Times*.

"Each of them has different attitudes relative to the positions and movement exacted by his work. That gait, this deportment, that manner of moving according to his trade—and always diverting—should be noted."

Delsarte, the nineteenth-century philosopher, formulated his laws of gesture only after many years of observation of the way in which human beings of all ages reacted to emotional stimuli. In his book *Every Little Movement*, Ted Shawn quotes Delsarte as saying:

"Gesture is more than speech. It is not what we say that persuades, but the manner of saying it. Speech is inferior to gesture because it corresponds to the phenomena of the mind. Gesture is the agent of the heart, the persuasive agent. That which demands a volume is uttered by a single word. A hundred pages do not say what a simple movement may express because the simple movement expresses our whole being."

In the twentieth century, Rudolf Laban formulated his philosophy through the same empirical approach and eventually developed a method of observing and recording movement which has enabled us to gain increasing insight into the importance of movement as an expression of inner impulses, reflecting temperament and mood.

In his chapter on expressive behaviour in *Pattern and Growth in Personality*, Allport writes of the studies carried out of such aspects of expression as posture, gesture, gait, hand-writing—termed "crystallised gesture"—facial movement, voice and speech. One hopes that, as Allport suggests, many other channels of expression will be explored by psychologists as well as by movement specialists.

It is because movement can be seen as the fundamental revelation and expression of individual personality that one can see dance, the art of movement, as a primary art. This is the heart of the argument.

Yet another reason for this thesis is that dance is the art which in the fullest measure expresses man's rhythmical nature. We see this in two ways. When excited or moved we show this in movement. Our speech may indicate our mood as we speak fluently, halt, stumble, vary the dynamics, raise or lower the pitch. We frequently reveal our feelings without speech. The mental pictures we have which recall children dancing with joy or rage are many. Those of adults are fewer. Yet one recalls such pictures as that of Bobby Moore, leaping and dancing, World Cup in hand. Not only do we reveal our feelings in rhythmical movement, pacing to and fro, rocking in pain or sorrow, jumping with excitement, but we can consider the reverse process. Participation in the rhythms of the dance can affect us and bring a new awareness of our powers. Joost Meerloo has written:

"Every dance is an unobtrusive attempt towards integration of movement. The symphony of rhythms is the choreography of life."

Dance is the art which in the fullest measure expresses man's rhythmical nature. By "the fullest measure" is implied the fact that the whole person is brought into play in a complete way. In comparing experiences in dance, in physical activities, in music, in painting, one finds that dance involves the whole person in an extraordinarily balanced way. There are stresses in individuals and stresses in types of dances but, allowing for this, no other activity demands so equally the use of the intellect, the body, the emotions and the intuition.

To sum up—dance can be considered as the primary art because, firstly, it is an expression in movement, which is itself the first expression of the human being; because, secondly, every other form of expression uses movement as its vehicle—sound making with voice or instrument, painting, sculpture, constructivism, dynamic architecture, kinetic art; because, thirdly, it is a form immediately conveyed in the body with no extension of brush, chisel, instrument; because, fourthly, dance springs from the universal language of movement which knows no barriers.

It follows that if dance is viewed in this way as the primary art, one must claim for it a place in the curriculum. It is clearly not a vocational subject, it has no utilitarian value, but perhaps, in an age that promises greater leisure for everyone, more attention should be paid to the aspects of education that are more concerned with fulfilling human potential, that is with "expression" as well as "coping."

CHAPTER 2

The place of dance in the middle school

IN writing of the importance of dance as a means of fostering artistic
expression, and of the special part that it can play because of the universal
and primary nature of the human being's expression of personality through
his movement, the need to use this activity as a balance to the academic
demands was considered of paramount importance in the secondary school.
These values are of course present in teaching any age group. In considering
the concept of the middle school one can see that dance could play a vital
role.

The opportunities offered by the middle school are considerable because
of the atmosphere which should prevail and which will surely be different
from the subject-stressed and more academic nature of much secondary
education, with transfer after selection at 11 plus, the emphasis on the examination syllabus and the consequent division of learning into isolated disci-
plines. When one examines the opportunities that a middle school offers, the
most important consideration is that of the possibility of the progressive
development of the child's abilities in movement throughout the very active
years from eight or nine to twelve or thirteen. In writing of the general
characteristics of children's movement during these years, one has of course
to admit that it is not yet possible to ascertain the effect upon the child of
transfer at these ages in terms of maturity, independence, responsibility and
group interplay. It is therefore only possible to draw upon experience in the
present junior and lower secondary schools. In general the eight-year-old is
full of vitality, able to comprehend and to use a wide range of movement
qualities, having considerable body awareness and the ability to respond to
others and to develop short dance phrases of his own. By ten he is able to use
combinations of qualities in basic effort actions and can work in a more
sensitive way with others to bring improvisations into a clear form. To do
this he brings to the activity his ability to concentrate for longer periods of
time.

19

Too often in the secondary school the teacher is laying foundations of dance experience such as have been mentioned as typical of achievement in the primary school. Children come to secondary schools from a large catchment area and only a few may have had any experience in dance. The same liveliness continues to be a strong characteristic of the lower secondary age group too. As a vocabulary is built up, dances of greater length are created and reveal evidence of mastery of movement and of creative powers. In the middle school the problems which many teachers associate with the third year in the secondary school would not arise. It is interesting to speculate in passing on the fact that indeed transfer at thirteen plus might eliminate the particular circumstances which make for problems with that age group.

In appreciating the scope for progression offered by the middle school to the children, it is important to realise the implication here. We are thinking of the boys as well as the girls. It must be regretted that for the vast majority of boys no opportunities are given to develop or to pursue this aspect of their education. When one sees the outstanding ability of junior boys and of those of secondary age who have had dance and dance drama experience, and when one sees similar qualities of concentration, invention, energy and humour in men students, it is difficult to understand why an aspect, so much a part of our lives, has been almost entirely excluded from boys' education.

Those in education responsible for setting up middle schools are able to start from first principles and establish a curriculum suitable for this particular age group, and aimed at satisfying the children's needs. This may provide opportunities for a fresh examination of the traditional, and often quite unrealistic, divisions into subjects thought appropriate to girls and another set thought suitable for boys. There is sufficient evidence of the valuable part that dance and dance drama has played in boys' education to encourage wider developments. In their book *Leap to Life* Wiles and Garrard give an account of their work in this field; in two schools in Worcester dance has been introduced in mixed and in boys' classes with successful results; in Hopefield Secondary School, Rathcoole, Co. Antrim, dance and dance drama has played a major role for many years. These are examples of work known personally to the writer and clearly could be added to. Nevertheless the introduction of dance into the curriculum for boys remains in the field of experiment in isolated schools rather than being evidence of a convinced and deliberate policy. The middle school could right this.

Team teaching will certainly be necessary if integration of subjects is to take place. There should be an exciting challenge for the teacher to bring to bear his particular knowledge of his subject discipline so that project work can be developed in depth.

There are two ways in which dance and dance drama can make a contribution. One way, already widespread, in which expressive movement has been used is in the field of dance mime. In this aspect of the art of movement we see the illustration of a story or a poem or an idea in terms of movement. So, for example, we may find used in this way such themes as Bonfire Night, A Volcano, The Sea, The Jabberwocky, David and Goliath. In his chapter on movement themes suitable for children in *Modern Educational Dance* Laban makes the point that dance plays with a story should be used sparingly. He writes:

"... the experience of movement imagination and memory of movement is a stimulus strong enough to make longer combinations of themes into movement studies interesting and enjoyable for the children."

The second way in which expressive movement can make a contribution as an integrating factor in the child's education is through the development of his mastery of the language of movement and appreciation of its universal nature. It is not simply that links can be made with other subjects such as religious knowledge, history and literature. Nor is it that dance drama can serve the need to provide another means of establishing understanding of verbal ideas, although this it may well do. Doubtless the participation in a dance drama based upon St. Francis may give greater insight into attitudes than any amount of intellectual discourse.

Integration, however, can be seen at a deeper level. One aim of education must be to encourage the capacity to see relationships and it is in this connection that movement education can play a part. This most basic form of expression can be developed as a prime means of comprehending the common factors in our varied experiences of the environment and of appreciating the relationship between the various manifestations of the child's creative impulses. In these common factors is included *rhythm* which is comprehended immediately in the body in stepping, in leaping, in rising and sinking, in action and recovery. Another factor is *form* which is comprehended immediately in the body in the shape of a gesture, in symmetry and asymmetry, in the shape of the body in action and in stillness, in the pathways created in moving from one place to another. The third factor is *relationship* which is comprehended immediately in the body in the relatedness of parts of the body to each other, in relationship with others in the pair, in the trio, in the group situation. These three factors which have just been described—rhythm, form and relationship— also occur in other types of creative activity. It is self-evident that each of them plays its part as a significant element in music, in the visual arts, in poetry, in mathematics and in science.

It is because the body is our most immediate instrument of expression that we can experience all these common factors—rhythm, form and rela- tionship—in a vital way through dance. So dance can serve not only to enrich and illuminate knowledge gained by other means but also as an art form in its own right, with a special integrating role.

Used in this way, dance could contribute to a balanced, diversified and integrated programme, such as Munro advocated, and so serve to enrich the children's powers of sense perception, imagination and sensitivity.

With transfer to secondary education at twelve or thirteen, pupils with a sound basis of movement mastery and dance experience could progress to the more advanced themes. In such an organisation as this, it might well be that a system of options could be given so that those for whom dance had provided a satisfying outlet could forge ahead in individual and group projects making dance and dance drama compositions of their own devising. In this way themes could be selected and the work carried out with help and guidance from the teacher. This sort of approach generates enthusiastic collaboration and involvement, attitudes which it is vital to encourage with senior pupils.

In planning a scheme of work suitable for the middle school, it is suggested that the material presented in *Creative Dance in the Primary School* should form the basis for the younger children of eight to eleven. The eleven to twelve and the twelve to thirteen age groups would then be able to progress to cover the material set out in Chapters 5 and 6 in this book.

There seems little doubt that in a middle school, with such a continuous scheme of dance teaching as outlined above, the rate of progress for the eleven- to thirteen-year-olds would be greater than for those pupils who start dance at eleven plus. The degree of progress remains to be assessed in the next few years when more schools of this type have been established with, one hopes, dance being given an integral place in the curriculum.

CHAPTER 3

Introducing dance in the secondary school

THERE are two principal ways in which a teacher can introduce dance into the secondary school. The teacher may start with the first year intake, or with both first and second years, and gradually build up the subject through the school over the years. The other plan is that all classes in the various age groups may start simultaneously, regardless of previous experience.

The advantage of the first scheme is that the difficulties involved in the introduction of new work to the third years and those above are avoided. Thus the teacher may avoid wrestling with the possible negative reactions and the lack of ability of those who have not experienced dance before. Disadvantages exist, however. Dance can easily be thought of as a subject suitable only for the younger children and as something to be dropped after the first two years. This view of dance may well be reinforced in a school by the rapid turn-over of teachers with a reluctance to embark on dance with the older children.

The advantages of starting dance throughout the school simultaneously are that the subject is seen to be considered suitable for all age groups and that the teacher can begin to form some ideas of ability and attitude throughout the school.

In general there is no problem in starting the subject in the first two years. In starting work with the first year intake it must be assumed that the children's background will be very varied. In a few cases they may have some background to draw on but the majority will have little experience of creative dance so that they will be meeting a new subject.

It must be emphasised that at whatever age dance is introduced, including adults, simple fundamental ideas must form the basis of the material so that a thorough foundation of experience and understanding is laid. For this reason the material which one might hope had been covered in the junior school must be introduced at this stage. The suggestions made for years 1 and 2 therefore cover the movement themes 1–8 as drawn up by Laban. Clearly progress will be faster when these themes are introduced at the secondary school level.

If dance is being taken for the first time in the second year then material suggested for year 1 must be presented first, progressing to the material suggested for year 2 as soon as the earlier work is familiar.

Many teachers find the third years in a secondary modern school the most difficult year to handle. There is certainly evidence to support the fact that it can be a difficult age group for an inexperienced teacher to introduce dance to. Indeed it can be very challenging and demanding for an experienced teacher. Once again the basic foundations must be laid. It cannot be reiterated too often that all those who have participated in this experiment are of the strong view that the early themes suggested for years 1 and 2 must have been experienced before further progress can be made to the material set out in the syllabus under the third year scheme. When introducing the simpler themes to third years the approach may well be different from that used with first and second years. The speed at which material is covered may also be faster. It is clear from this that the movement vocabulary and standard of attainment in such a third year cannot reach that of a third year with two years' experience behind them. It is, for example, useless to think that a third year could perform a dimensional space study when they have not fully experienced and comprehended in the body the spatial actions of rising and sinking, opening and crossing and advancing and retreating.

In introducing simple movement ideas one significant difference of approach between the method used with first years and that used with third years has been noted. The first years are happy to work in an exploratory way and build simple movement "conversations" and short dance phrases. The third years, on the other hand, seem to need to develop simple material into short dances which are strongly based on relationship and can be completed in one lesson. This approach has proved successful in gaining the interest and participation of "difficult" third year groups for whom dance is a new subject.

A similar approach is helpful to those beginning dance in the fourth, fifth and sixth years, although they seem to present less of a problem than third years. Discussion seems to show that the difficulties associated with third years in a secondary modern school, where the majority of pupils are in their penultimate year, tend to occur with fourth years in the selective grammar schools where most pupils are staying into the fifth year. Problems have been encountered in introducing dance to fourth years in a secondary school when the pupils are due to leave in six months' time. This is, however, undoubtedly bound up with the whole question of an appropriate programme, including choice, for leavers.

Fifth and sixth formers can have their interest aroused through a realisation of the significance of movement in human expression. They can become involved in appreciating the relationship between verbal expression, with which they are more familiar, and movement expression. The common interest in rhythm in these two forms can be comprehended. This point strikes one immediately in reading Dame Edith Sitwell's comments on her poetry in her autobiography *Taken Care Of.* She writes:

"From the thin, glittering, occasionally shadowed, airy, ever-varying texture of that miracle of poetry, the instinct was instilled in me that not only structure, but also texture, are parents of rhythm in poetry, and that variations in speed are the result, not only of structure, but also of texture."

Writing of the poems in *Facade* she says:

"The technical experiments in these poems consist, for the most part, of enquiries into the effect on rhythm and on speed of the use of rhymes, assonances and dissonances placed not only at the end of the lines, but at the beginning, and in different and most elaborate patterns throughout the verse, and, too, there are enquiries into the effect on speed of equivalent syllables. By this I mean that if you use one three-syllabled word it has greater speed than the three one-syllabled words which might have been used as its equivalent. The use of two rhymes placed immediately together at the end of each of two lines, sound like leaps into the air. . . . Some of the poems appeared to have a violent exhilaration, others have a veiled melancholy, a sadness masked by gaiety."

The interest in rhythm, which could well be aroused in a senior class

26

through such ideas and experiments as those discussed above, might well provide a starting-point for experiments in movement rhythms.

Older boys and girls will also be able to appreciate the common elements of texture, form and design that are perceived in the visual arts as well as experienced in movement. A teacher wishing to make this a starting-point might refer to such a book as *Elements of the Art of Architecture* by William Muschenheim. His writing in the chapter on "Form" in which he deals with the elements that produce the static balance of formal harmony, the dynamic composition of formal contrast, with the tension between opposites, and the significance of directional emphasis, could provide a point of departure in interesting a group in the similar results in movement expression.

Music is clearly very easily related to dance and it may well be that a class may have their interest in movement stirred by the chance to move to music they particularly enjoy. In this case the movement will probably be poor in content but, if the motivation is there, it will be possible to improve the quality.

Where a school has a strong drama department or a tradition of dramatic presentations, the interest of the fifth and sixth years can be gained through an exploration of the dramatic element in movement. While it is not wise to embark on lengthy dance dramas, reference to the familiar is most valuable. Thus an understanding can be built up of the significance of posture, gesture and action in characterisation in drama and in dramatic situations. Simple material can be introduced in this way within a familiar context. For example, in taking a workshop session with a mixed group of teenagers at a theatre club, simple ideas of travelling, leaping, arresting the movement, of groups advancing and retreating in opposition to each other, of encircling, of leaders encountering each other with firm grip—all this with firm stepping and tension in the body—caught their interest and gained their enthusiasm and respect. One cannot be blind to the fact that the legend of dance being for cissies and concerned with moving trees dies a slow death.

If long stories are worked out, completing the story can easily become the dominant factor and movement experience remain of secondary importance. If, however, the dramatic implications in particular movement experiences are emphasised, then a more creative situation can be brought about. Thus

27

the possibilities of contrast, of change, of unusual development can be explored and the dramatic element perceived. Examples can be included under the headings of the body, effort quality, space, as well as in the more obvious category of relationship. Within the aspect of *body action* some of the following suggestions have been used. Contrast can be experienced between the fluent, continuous travelling about the space in which changes of direction are gradual and curved and turning pathways are used, and the sudden stops and the sharp changes of direction from which emerge interrupted, broken flow and zigzag pathways—a less harmonious form of expression. Natural succession of flow of movement through the body, for example shoulder, elbow, wrist, hand, can be contrasted with such unusual successions as shoulder, wrist, elbow, hand, which produces a grotesque expression. Incidentally, the sequences which can come from individuals approaching with such successive movements, in legs as well as arms, the group relating to each other and surrounding the common centre will be far more original than the results gained from, say, a trolls' dance to Grieg's music "In the Hall of the Mountain King," where preconceived ideas may dominate.

All sorts of possibilities can be explored within the theme of body awareness with meeting and parting, leading and following, making contact of body parts. Groups might use the same body part or each person could choose a different one; all could take a succession of movements with first one, then another and then a third body part. The results could be grotesque, full of tension or of a comic nature. The opposition felt in the pulling apart of body parts into opposite directions—such as one arm high and the other deep or hands crossing over into the opposite areas—could be developed into pair or trio sequences in which this counter-tension is experienced. Rhythmic developments can take place and interplay can be developed and form a beginning which could be resolved in many different ways by the class. Through such an approach the simple themes can be introduced with a strong emphasis on relationship and in a manner likely to interest older children. The results may be in the nature of movement conversations, and not yet dances, but the pupils are coming to terms with the art of movement and its significance in social interactions.

The field of *effort* is a rich one for this sort of approach. Within this aspect experiment can be made of the response of one individual to another using contrasting effort qualities or combinations of these. The reaction of one individual to another's clear effort action could start off a response sequence. The contrast could be experienced between lively energetic leaps, steps and turns and gentle travelling, rising, sinking and turning. A group using predominantly sustained efforts could react to one using sudden efforts; three groups employing pressing–wringing rhythms, gliding–floating rhythms and dabbing–flicking rhythms could develop a dance play in which all manner of developments of interaction and of subsequent floor pattern could be evolved.

These are but a few examples from an extensive field of effort contrasts and combinations.

The dramatic possibilities inherent in the use of *space* can be explored. In this aspect the contrast felt between constricted movement in a small area of space, in which possibly only small pulsating or vibrating movements or turning on the spot was possible, could be contrasted with the feeling of breadth and expansion experienced in a spreading or leaping or travelling movement encompassing a great amount of space. This could be experienced by individuals or by groups. A phrase of movement, in which a tightly closed group eventually increased the distance between them until they broke away from each other, became aware of their isolation and returned again to the group, is an example of a movement sequence of dramatic significance. This could be compared with a more fluent and rhythmical play between near and far with the group which might be of a more dance-like nature. Contrasting air patterns in the space have their particular movement significance. Thus an individual or group approach using angular gestures encountering another using more curving pathways, or another using the deviating pathways of a twisted pattern, will produce reactions of a dramatic nature.

Many possibilities lie within the interplay of those moving at different levels. It is significant that associations exist between height and heaven, aspiration, goodness, freedom of the air, life, power. Depth has been associated with hell, despair, evil, earthbound, death, submission. Clearly then in any free play using high and deep levels, contrasts, oppositions and conflicts will arise. Thus beginners can appreciate the difference in expression between rising and sinking with eyes uplifted, rising and sinking with eyes focused on the ground, rising with eyes uplifted and sinking with eyes downward, and vice versa. The body parts leading the movement and the effort quality employed will additionally affect the expression of the movement. The individual will experience something different if, on the one hand, he starts on the ground, rises with a firm, sustained action to his feet only to collapse to the floor again, while, on the other hand, he rises lightly and suddenly and subsides with sustainment. The opposite poles of high and deep present ideal opportunities for pair and inter-group relationships. Changes can take place simultaneously; the deep can be drawn up; the high pulled down; steps, turns and jumps can bring about floor patterns. New possibilities occur when the medium level is included and tripartite possibilities occur with the introduction of an intermediary between the extremes.

The spatial actions of advancing and retreating clearly hold possibilities for similar response sequences. Even without stressing a particular choice of effort quality, the implications of an advancing gesture or step answered by a similar action, differ from the advance countered by a retreat and differs again from a common retreat. Clearly there is much to be explored when one thinks of the difference between a rushing advance answered by a turning hasty retreat, and a hesitant halting advance answered by sustained retreat, to give only two examples.

Again, the spatial actions of crossing and opening can form the basis for simple sequences. The sensation of cutting oneself off from others in a crossing action is contrasted with the more exposed situation of an opening action. Thus, for example, different situations will occur if one person gradually closes across himself while his partner makes an opening movement, or if they both close and both open at the same time. If a person encourages his partner to spread from a closed starting position with or without real touch, a dramatic relationship will occur, as it will if partners close in towards each other and then spread away, either together or one after another.

Within the realm of *relationship* the dramatic element is particularly evident. The pair situation in itself has a polarity so that alternate action, action and response, counter-action, meeting and parting are in themselves full of potential. Equally the trio promotes scope with its triangular implications, and the "two against one" alignments possible. The possibilities of

30

larger groups can be explored. An individual motif on, say, opening and closing performed near others can provide a stimulating starting-point for further developments. Groups relating to other groups have already been mentioned. There are new group formation possibilities, each with their own characters, to be tried out. Thus the loose group, the closely knotted group, the wedge, the wall, the circle all have their own expressive power.

These very simple ideas have been suggested as possible starting-points for older girls and boys who may have an interest in drama or in human movement generally. So many references can be made by the teachers to everyday situations which share something of this fundamental interplay: the strikes, the riots, the confrontations of nations, have elements in common with the group situations mentioned and reference can be made to this without necessarily embarking on a full-scale representation of the event. Such work serves as an introduction to symbolic action which is our main concern. As Laban wrote:

> "Many people, perhaps a greatly increasing number of people, feel that our working lives are as full as our dreams of symbolic actions, and that some medium is needed in which actions of this kind can find aesthetic expression. That medium is obviously to be found in that area of movement which we call dance and mime."

If the teacher new to the school can draw on the interest created by established teachers, or on pieces of work in other fields which the pupils have found exciting, this will compensate for the lack of movement experience and provide a background which will give them confidence. In helping seniors to appreciate the common elements in the arts the teacher of dance can play a valuable part. It is most unlikely that another member of the staff will make references to the relationship between their particular discipline and movement, and so it rests with the dance teacher to do this. In helping older children to use more than their intellectual capacities the kind of approach is similar to that used with students in their first year of training. Through sending them out to make observations of people carrying out everyday and working actions; through the observations of posture and gesture in conversation; through delving into poetry and prose for examples of rhythm and vivid description of action; through collecting pictures and materials of contrasting texture, density and shape; through searching for music of contrasting mood—an awareness can be developed of the universality of movement in all forms of life and human expression.

CHAPTER 4

Thinking in terms of movement: an analysis

IF we wish to study movement, then we must observe human beings in action. Whether observing a child at play, a man's everyday or working actions, a skilled performer or a dancer, we can make an analysis of the movement under certain headings. In fact we tend to observe the unified whole, but by specific observation of one aspect or another a detailed analysis can be made.

The four main headings under which we observe movement are:

1. The body
2. Effort
3. Space and shape
4. Relationship

If we take each of these in turn we shall be able to discover a number of interesting factors under each heading. In order to appreciate the validity of this analysis it would be best for the reader to observe a number of people, children or adults, in action in a variety of situations and so become aware of these various factors.

The body

This one might think of as the *structure* with which the activity is performed, the body being the *instrument* of expression. Thus we differentiate:

1. BODY ACTIVITY

We can observe what *activity* is being performed. This may be:

(a) *Locomotion* of some kind—for example, stepping, running, rolling— with the intention of travelling along the surface of the floor in some way. Steps may vary in extension, may be at deep, high or medium level, may be on different parts of the foot and can create varied pathways over the floor.

C

(b) *Elevation*—hopping, skipping, leaping, jumping, using the five basic possibilities of jumping—from one foot to the same foot; from one foot to the other; from both to both; from both to one and from one to both—travelling upwards with the intention of leaving the floor and flying up into or through the air. Jumps may achieve great height, may be bouncing in rhythm, may be at a deep level, as is often seen in the men's dance in Russian ensembles. Feet and legs may be extended and far apart or they may be near or even touch during the jump. Thus different body shapes will be achieved.

(c) *Turns*—spinning, pivoting, whirling around, with the intention of constantly changing front. Participation in this action serves to bring about a sense of integration as the environment is taken in in one action and the mover becomes the centre of his "world." Turning is one of the actions that enhances the feeling of flow. Turning may be brought about through pivoting on the spot, through a leg gesture which causes the standing leg to turn, through gathering and scattering arm gestures, through a jump, through rapid steps on the spot, through describing a curved pathway on the floor, through a change of front in the body when the feet are placed one in front of the other.

(d) *Gesture*—shaping movements in the air with the arms or legs, gathering, scattering and penetrating the space, without any transference of weight. A gathering gesture creates a three-dimensional trace form in which the movement starts at a distance from and finishes close to the centre of the body. A scattering gesture is a three-dimensional trace form in which the movement starts near to and finishes away from the centre of the body. A penetrating gesture travels through the space in a one-dimensional stress describing a straight pathway. Gestures may be performed with simultaneous or successive action of the limbs; they may use the many possible directions and levels; they may precede a step or follow a step; their form may be angular, curved or twisted; arm and leg gesture may take place in unison or one may follow the other; extension of the gesture will bring about enlargement of the trace form and may cause the dancer to leave the original stance and thus execute floor patterns.

(e) *Rising and sinking*—the rising action has the intention of reaching upwards, of striving for the greatest possible distance of one's body from the ground, pulling against gravity. The sinking action goes with the pull of gravity as the body drops, sinks, collapses, presses itself into the ground. Rising has an association with aspiration. In colloquial language we refer to "climbing the ladder to success," "rising above one's difficulties," "feeling uplifted," the "spirit soaring." Similarly sinking holds connotations of despair. We speak of "being in the depths," "feeling bogged down," having that "sinking feeling," the "heart dropping."

(f) *Opening and crossing*—in opening there is the intention of broadening the body, reaching with the arms and legs to their own side and so stressing the openness and width in the body. In crossing there is a contraction, a folding, as the limbs reach across the body and arrive in a situation where all parts of the body are near to each other. In the open situation the mover is enabled to be aware of others while in the crossed situation the closed limbs serve to protect or cut off the mover from others.

(g) *Advancing and retreating*—in advancing, the body reaches forward, using gestures of the arms with the intention of moving onwards. In retreating there is a drawing backwards with the intention of withdrawal. The onward moving indicates progression into a future state as eyes, front of the body, gesture, all lead forward. The backward moving indicates retrogression and a return to a past state as the steps, back of the body, gesture, all lead in the opposite direction from that of the vision.

2. BODY PARTS

We can observe which *parts* of the body are actively involved in the movement. These may be shown diagrammatically, as illustrated (p. 36).

We may observe whether the movement takes place in the body as a whole, as in travelling, flying or falling, or whether it takes place in particular areas or joints, as in the knees or arms or head. We can pay attention to what the less active body parts are doing—remaining relatively inactive, echoing the main movements, working in opposition.

3. BODY SYMMETRY

We can observe the *symmetry* or *asymmetry* of the body—whether both sides are moving similarly or one side is particularly emphasised by, for example, a gesture of arm or leg, or a drop or a lift of the side. A symmetric shape is more stable, secure and calm; an asymmetric one is mobile, exciting and stimulating.

4. BODY FLOW

We can observe the *flow* of movement in the body and note whether it is simultaneous or successive. In simultaneous movement the action occurs in all the joints and body parts at the same time. In successive movement

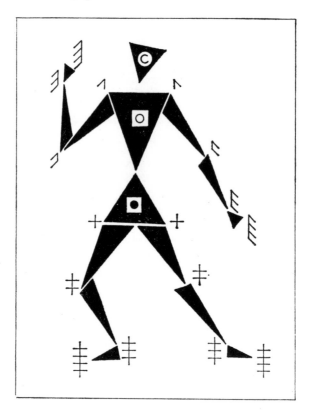

the action flows through from one joint and part to another and then another, e.g. shoulder, elbow, wrist, hand.

5. BODY SHAPE

We can observe the *shape* of the body as it crystallises in stillness. These shapes can be categorised as:

(a) *Arrow-like:* one-dimensional: in a single directional stress. This is most easily experienced when lying in an elongated position, in the end position which results from a direct rising action and, to a limited extent, when both arms take up the same directional pull while one leg reaches into the opposite direction. Clearly in this case the standing leg takes on a secondary direction.

(b) *Wall-like:* two-dimensional: with height and depth. The position is usually achieved as a result of a flat, spreading action in which the symmetry of the right and left sides is accentuated and in which the body divides the space around it into a front and a back area.

(c) *Ball-like:* three-dimensional: of curved and rounded nature. This shape is achieved as a result of an action in which the head, knees and arms are drawn together. It may be arrived at from a gathering, turning and sinking action or from a curling of the spine.

(d) *Screw-like:* three-dimensional: of twisted nature. This shape is achieved through the counter-pull of the extremities of the body as they turn and twist in opposition.

Effort: how the body moves

Here we are concerned with the attitude of the mover to the motion factors of weight, time, space and flow.

1. WEIGHT

We can observe the use of *weight* in an action. This may be *either* firm, strong, gripped, weighty *or* fine touch, delicate, light, airborne, buoyant.

2. TIME

We can observe the *time* taken in an action. This may be *either* sudden, quick, hasty, hurried, momentary, of short duration *or* sustained, slow, leisurely, unhurried, prolonged, of long duration.

3. SPACE

We can observe the space pathway followed in an action. This may be *either* direct, straight, undeviating, threadlike, of unilateral extension *or* flexible, wavy, roundabout, plastic, pliant, of multilateral extension.

37

4. FLOW

We can observe the *flow* of the action. This may be *either* bound, controlled, readily stopped *or* free, fluent, streaming onwards, abandoned.

Compounds of a quality of weight with one of time and one of space were termed by Laban *basic effort actions* and are set out as follows to show their relationship.

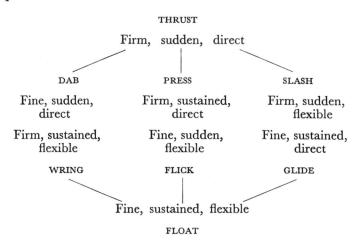

THRUST
Firm, sudden, direct

DAB	PRESS	SLASH
Fine, sudden, direct	Firm, sustained, direct	Firm, sudden, flexible
Firm, sustained, flexible	Fine, sudden, flexible	Fine, sustained, direct
WRING	FLICK	GLIDE

Fine, sustained, flexible

FLOAT

Space and shape : where the body moves

Here we are concerned with the shaping of the movement in the space.

1. EXTENSION

We can observe the *size* of a movement, which may be:

(a) Small (near to the body), or
(b) Large (far from the body),

or degrees between.

2. LEVEL

We may observe the *level* into which the movement travels. This may be:

(a) High.
(b) Medium.
(c) Deep.

When considering the whole body in action, *high* level refers to the area above the shoulder girdle. This is most naturally used by the arms and it is penetrated in leaping and jumping. The *deep* level refers to the area below the hips. This is most naturally used by the legs and is entered in crouching, sitting, kneeling and lying. The *medium* level refers to the area between shoulders and hips which is most naturally used in turning.

3. DIRECTION

We may observe the *direction* towards which the movement travels. Certain directions will be penetrated as a result of particular activities. Thus rising and sinking will travel towards high and deep, opening and crossing will travel towards the right and left sides, advancing and retreating will travel towards forward and backward.

More complex activities will travel towards other directions. A movement, with the right side leading, which simultaneously rises and opens will lead into the direction high-right, while a counter-movement which sinks and crosses will lead into deep-left; one which sinks and opens will lead into the direction deep-right, while a counter-movement which rises and crosses will lead into high-left. The peripheral, circular pathway which links these four points of orientation, high-right, high-left, deep-right and deep-left, has been referred to as "the door plane."

A movement, with the right side leading, which simultaneously opens and advances will lead into the direction right-forward, while a counter-movement which crosses and retreats will lead into left-backward; one which opens and retreats will lead into the direction right-backward, while a counter movement which crosses and advances will lead into left-forward. The peripheral, circular pathway which links these four points of orientation, right-forward, right-backward, left-backward and left-forward, has been referred to as "the table plane".

A movement which simultaneously advances and sinks will lead into the direction forward-deep, while a counter-movement which retreats and rises will lead into backward-high; a movement which retreats and sinks will lead into the direction backward-deep, while a counter-movement which advances and rises will lead into forward-high. The peripheral, circular pathway which links these four points of orientation, forward-deep, forward-

39

high, backward-high and backward-deep, has been referred to as "the wheel plane."

It follows that three such activities carried out simultaneously will lead into diagonal directions. Thus, to give two examples, a movement, using the right side, which simultaneously rises, opens and advances will lead into the diagonal direction high-right-forward, while a counter-movement which sinks, crosses and retreats will lead into deep-left-backward. The other six diagonal directions can be arrived at in a similar manner.

Thus, using the right side:

rising, crossing and advancing
 will lead into the direction high-left-forward
sinking, opening and retreating
 will lead into the direction deep-right-backward
rising, opening and retreating
 will lead into the direction high-right-backward
sinking, crossing and advancing
 will lead into the direction deep-left-forward
rising, crossing and retreating
 will lead into the direction high-left-backward
sinking, opening and advancing
 will lead into the direction deep-right-forward

4. AIR PATTERN

We may observe the *air pattern* created by a movement. The pattern traced in the air may be:

(a) Straight.
(b) Angular.
(c) Curved.
(d) Twisted.

An angular shape stresses the sharp change of direction and, in execution, brings into play the need to bind and then to free the flow of movement in order to achieve this change. A curved pattern uses a gradual change of direction and is related to a centre which is being surrounded. Clearly, the further the curve progresses the more obvious is this relationship until, with the shaping of a circle, the surrounding of the centre is completed. The expression of a circle is that of wholeness and unity created by the smooth, rounded pathway and by the return to the first point of departure. A spiral pathway keeps this rounded nature but gains an added expression from either the increase or decrease in size of the progression through the space. A twisted pattern involves continual changes of direction as the pathway traced surrounds one centre after another.

5. FLOOR PATTERN

We can observe whether the movement takes place in the space immediately around the body or whether it extends into the general space of the room. We may observe the *floor pattern* which arises. This also may be in the form of a straight, angular, curved or twisted path.

Relationship

1. RELATIONSHIP OF BODY PARTS

We may observe the relationship of *parts of the body* to each other in action or when the movement crystallises into stillness and there is more awareness of body shape.

2. RELATIONSHIP OF INDIVIDUALS

We may observe the relationship of *dancers to each other*. We may observe them near, apart, approaching, parting, surrounding, by the side of, in front of, behind, leading, following; moving in unison, in canon, in opposition, in harmony.

3. RELATIONSHIP OF GROUPS

We may observe the relationship of *groups to each other*, as above in 2.

This analysis can be summarised as shown on pages 42 and 43.

This analysis serves in many ways. Firstly, it is a guide to help the teacher to look more closely and specifically at movement, serving as a framework upon which to base observations of movement. Moreover, because of its fundamental character it can be used as a basis for looking at any movement —everyday actions, working actions, physical activities and expressive activities.

SUMMARY OF ANALYSIS

Aspect 1
THE BODY
WHAT

1. Activity
     (a) Locomotion
     (b) Elevation
     (c) Turns
     (d) Gesture
     (e) Rising, sinking
     (f) Opening, crossing
     (g) Advancing, retreating

2. Body part used

3. Symmetry or asymmetry

4. Body flow—
   simultaneous or
   successive

5. Body shape
     (a) Arrow
     (b) Wall
     (c) Ball
     (d) Screw

Aspect 2
EFFORT
HOW

Motion factors	Qualities
1. Weight	Firm
	Fine touch
2. Time	Sudden
	Sustained
3. Space	Direct
	Flexible
4. Flow	Bound
	Free

BASIC EFFORT ACTIONS

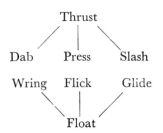

Thrust

Dab   Press   Slash

Wring   Flick   Glide

Float

FOUR ASPECTS

Aspect 3
SPACE
WHERE

Aspect 4
RELATIONSHIP
WITH

1. Extension

    (a) Small (near)
    (b) Large (far)

1. Relatedness of body parts to each other

2. Level

    (a) High
    (b) Medium
    (c) Deep

2. Relationship of individuals to each other

3. Directions

High . . .	Deep
Right . . .	Left
Forward . .	Backward

3. Relationship of groups to each other

High-right . .	Deep-left
Deep-right . .	High-left
Right-forward· .	Left-backward
Right-backward .	Left-forward
Forward-deep .	Backward-high
Backward-deep .	Forward-high

High-right-forward .	Deep-left-backward
High-left-forward .	Deep-right-backward
High-left-backward .	Deep-right-forward
High-right-backward .	Deep-left-forward

4. Air pattern
    (a) Straight line
    (b) Angular shape
    (c) Curved shape
    (d) Twisted shape

5. Floor pattern
    (as above)

43

This analysis

Such a guide is clearly a valuable aid to any teacher and not only to the movement specialist. The classroom teacher can become aware of the mood of the class, can observe more specifically the body posture and movement characteristics being used and can adapt his attitude accordingly. Thus, for example, a teacher arriving to take a class which is talkative and fidgety would do well to participate in this excited mood by darting quick-fire questions which require immediate response. From such a beginning he can put questions which require increasing thought until he establishes a mood of concentration, if he so wishes. The teacher will also be aware of the movement characteristics of each child. So he may appreciate what is at the basis of distinctions between children who may be termed slow and careful, excitable and bubbly, anxious and fussy, controlled and calm, quiet and neat, awkward and clumsy.

Secondly, this analysis serves as the basis from which our material for movement teaching can be selected and so is a help in planning lessons and schemes. Although we make such an analysis for clarification and observation, in fact there is a synthesis of these aspects in bodily action—the body performs rhythmic action in space. Because of this wholeness, many varied starting-points can be used.

A third use of this analysis of movement is that it provides a good framework for the teacher to have in mind when helping the child to develop his own understanding and observation of movement. As one child watches another, he can become increasingly aware of the possibilities and general principles underlying quite diverse individual movement phrases and sequences and, later, dances. It may be, for example, noting whether the jumps are off or on to one or two feet, noting the accent in a phrase, observing the levels through which the movement passes. These are all definite points for a child to observe and such specific observations have more purpose than his being asked to watch another child with no pointers to guide him in what to look for.

Further familiarity with the analysis enables the teacher to aid the children to develop and clarify their own movement sequences. This could take the form of drawing attention to the function of a less active part of the body, suggesting that the sequence needs clarifying from the point of view of stress or timing, or clarification of the levels and directions used.

So this analysis forms the basis upon which the movement vocabulary can be built. That various aspects are more suitable as starting-points for different age groups is of course true. This has been indicated by Laban in *Modern Educational Dance* in the chapters "Dancing through the Age Groups" and "Sixteen Basic Movement Themes."

The link between the sixteen themes suggested as appropriate for pupils of secondary age and the analysis of the four aspects already tabulated is summarised as follows:

Theme 1. Themes concerned with the awareness of the body—*body aspect*.

Theme 2. Themes concerned with the awareness of force and time—*effort aspect*.

Theme 3. Themes concerned with the awareness of space—*space aspect*.

Theme 4. Themes concerned with the awareness of the flow of the weight of the body in space and time—*effort aspect*.

Theme 5. Themes concerned with the adaptation to partners—*relationship aspect*.

Theme 6. Themes concerned with the instrumental use of the limbs of the body—*body aspect*.

Theme 7. Themes concerned with the awareness of isolated actions—*effort aspects*.

Theme 8. Themes concerned with occupational rhythms—*effort and body aspects*.

Theme 9. Themes concerned with the shapes of movement—*space aspect*.

Theme 10. Themes concerned with combinations of the eight basic actions—*effort aspect*.

Theme 11. Themes concerned with space orientation—*space aspect*.

Theme 12. Themes concerned with the performance of shapes and efforts by different parts of the body—*body, effort and space aspects*.

Theme 13. Themes concerned with elevation from the ground—*body aspect*.

Theme 14. Themes concerned with the awakening of group feeling—*relationship and effort aspects*.

Theme 15. Themes concerned with group formations—*relationship and space aspects.*

Theme 16. Themes concerned with the expressive qualities or moods of movements—*body, effort, space and relationship aspects.*

CHAPTER 5

First Year Secondary, aged 11—12

The structure of the syllabus

In the detailed syllabus for the secondary school that follows, the four aspects of the body, effort, space and relationship are covered with cross-references to the sixteen basic movement themes as put forward by Laban. Although the syllabus has been set out in age groups, it must be stressed that this is intended only as a guide to progression in suitable material and is in no way binding or a rigid plan. All that can be claimed is that all the material included has been found useful and has led to successful dance experience with the stated age group.

In order to formulate the syllabus, a skeleton scheme was drawn up based on the writer's personal teaching experience with these age groups. The scheme was tried out in one chosen school for twelve months with the co-operation of a teacher new to the school. At the end of the year, a group of secondary teachers met together to discuss the content of a syllabus using as a basis the original scheme, with adaptations made during the year. During the succeeding two years, reports came back on the apparent suitability or otherwise of the suggested material. Concurrently, the work in the original school continued with regular teaching and recorded observation taking place. It will be clear that the most valuable observation of third year response took place in the third year of the experiment when the pupils had been working progressively with the same teacher since they entered the school. This was in no way a scientifically drawn-up piece of research. There is room for much investigation of that kind and there seems little doubt that with the inclusion of dance as one of the subjects in the B.Ed. Degrees such detailed studies will take place.

At this stage, however, the need is for more dance teaching in the secondary schools. The intention is therefore to give suggestions which are the result of practical experience on the part of actual teachers in a school situation, and which are likely to prove successful and of help to students and less experienced teachers. It is important that newly qualified teachers embark on the teaching of dance immediately they start in their first teaching post while their personal experience is still fresh. This is vital if we are to correct the all too prevalent situation whereby many children have only a year or so of dance before the teacher leaves. The rapid turn-over of teachers in recent years has tended to make dance a subject for first years and sixth form clubs. This is no way demonstrates the con-tribution that the subject can make.

First Year Secondary, 11–12 years

Characteristics of this age group are its unselfconscious involvement in a movement experience, its ability to invent sequences of its own and its great enjoyment and sense of achievement in doing so. To give opportunities to succeed and thus gain in confidence is particularly important for children of this age who have failed the eleven plus or who are in the lower streams in a school. Spontaneity is easily aroused at this age and is balanced by a desire to repeat dances they have worked out.

BODY AWARENESS—LABAN THEME I AND 6

Activities must be introduced as a basis upon which to build the children's feeling for quality. Thus they should become familiar with the possibilities inherent in locomotion, stepping, elevation, gesture, rising and sinking, opening and crossing, advancing and retreating and of the arresting of the flow of movement in stopping. These activities will not only be experienced as single actions but will also be used in combination. In this way they will build action rhythms using, for example, travelling and leaping, turning jumps, a gesture of the hand leading into rising or sinking or turning, spiralling turns which rise or sink.

Awareness of body shape will be gained from paying attention to the appropriate preparation and ending of phrases and sequences and to clari-fication of the relatedness of parts of the body to each other and to others.

48

Awareness of body parts must be stressed from the beginning since clarity in the part of the body used or leading an action will contribute considerably to meaningful movement. In laying these foundations the children should become aware of the particular function of the various body parts. They should be given opportunities to discover *the uses of the feet* in stepping, which would include steps of different levels, sizes and directions, the use of different parts of the feet, the part played by the foot in leg gestures and the rhythmical variations in the five basic jumps.

The part played by the *hands* will be evident in spreading and contracting arm gestures, in rising and sinking, advancing, retreating and turning actions led by the surfaces, edges or tips of the hands. Gripping, gathering, releasing, scattering and penetrating gestures of the hands can be enlarged to bring into play the whole body. Contrasts in touch can be felt in such relationship tasks as meeting with a firm grip or in jumping around a partner, using a firm hold, contrasted with careful leading of a partner or a momentary light touch before leaping away. Unusual succession in the use of the wrist and finger joints will bring about a grotesque expression. Hands will also be used in clapping and snapping or in beating the body to serve as a natural accompaniment.

An awareness of the use of the *knees* will be brought about through such actions as leaping and jumping, in deep stepping, in stepping in which the knee leads the gesture of the leg, in driving gestures from the centre of the body out into the space around.

The bent, angular nature of the knee joint can be compared with the similarly shaped *elbow* joint. Movements with the elbow can also be made with a thrusting penetration of the space. The inner and outer surfaces of the elbows can lead in a turning or in a rising or sinking gesture, thus forming clear air patterns. An expression of sharpness and angularity will be brought about when both elbows and knees are emphasised in lively action.

Awareness should also be gained of the possibilities of lifting, lowering, twisting, contracting and extending the whole *limb*, of the need for mobility in the spine, the shoulders and the hips, and of the appropriate participation of the whole body or its parts in a chosen action. The whole body will be used in such actions as rising, sinking, spreading, closing and changes between standing, sitting, lying and kneeling. The relatedness of active

D

parts will be realised both in such actions as listed above and also in such play activities as the meeting and parting of elbow and knee.

EFFORT—LABAN THEMES 2 AND 4

A foundation of understanding of movement quality must be laid through the experience and practice of the factors of weight, time, space and flow and simple combinations of these (see page 38).

WEIGHT—*firmness and fine touch*: experience of firmness is gained in stepping, jumping, "making a strong statue," gripping in towards the centre of the body, pressing up away from the floor, pressing down into the floor. Experience of fine touch is gained in stepping, in light jumps, in relaxing and opening from gripped positions. Grip and release can be combined in a phrase.

TIME—*suddenness and sustainment*: experience of suddenness can be gained in quick darting movements, sudden turns and jumps, quick gestures of hands. Experience of sustainment can be gained in the separating and meeting of the hands, in rising and sinking, in spreading and closing. Problems of balance make stepping with sustainment difficult.

SPACE—*directness and flexibility*: experience of directness is gained in travelling over the floor in straight pathways, in gestures cutting through the space. Experience of flexibility is gained in turning and twisting, in weaving in roundabout pathways through the space, in arm gestures involving the use of the space all around the body.

FLOW—*free and bound*: contrasts can be experienced between continuity in leaping and travelling, rolling and turning, on the one hand; and in travelling with a readiness to stop and in arresting the flow of movement in stopping, on the other.

Combinations of the qualities of weight, time and space can be made.
Firm and sudden qualities can be combined in the sudden gripping of the whole body, in energetic leaps which burst upwards into the air, in downward jumps stressing the accent into the floor, in explosive turning jumps, in the sharp shooting out of elbows, knees and feet and in rhythmical beating

and travelling with the feet. The beating of a drum or tambourine can be a helpful accompaniment.

Fine touch and sudden qualities can be combined in excited darting, flickering, quivering hand gestures, in the light shooting out and back of the feet, in the tapping of the floor with the feet, in hasty jumps, turns and travelling which give an experience of surprise or shock. Marraccas, skulls, castanets and bells can be helpful for accompaniment.

Firm and sustained qualities can be combined in slow contraction of the whole body, in the tension of pulling parts of the body away from each other, in the pressing together of body parts, in screwing down towards the ground, in turning and twisting using backs, shoulders and elbows, in pressing out into the space using hands and other body parts to lead. It is difficult to get sustained strength with percussion sound but a continuous strong drum beat can sometimes be helpful.

Fine touch and sustained qualities can be combined in gentle spreading and turning of the whole body, in "airborne" rising, in smoothing, waving, undulating gestures of the hands and as a transition to relaxation after firm, sustained action as above. The soft playing of a large cymbal or gong, a shaken tambourine, a xylophone, or smoothing the parchment of a drum can be helpful as accompaniment.

Direct and firm qualities can be combined in forceful, boring, cleaving, penetrating gestures through the space using finger-tips, fists, elbows, soles of feet and in downward driving with feet stressing powerful, purposeful action.

Direct and fine touch qualities can be combined in gentle smoothing gestures which glide rather than bore through the space and in skimming across the floor from place to place.

Direct and sudden qualities can be combined in shooting upwards from a crouched position on the floor, in gestures using fingers, elbows and feet to pierce the space with definite focus and aim, in jumps straight up into the air and pouncing down on to a spot on the floor.

Direct and sustained qualities can be combined in slow upward rising with emphasis on the gradual threading of the body straight through the space. It can be experienced in slow, clear-cut gestures using the finger-tips or edge of the hand, in unhurried, purposeful stepping in an undeviating pathway.

Flexible and firm qualities can be combined in screwing, twisting arm and leg gestures which use counter-tension and in the turning, twisting and knotting of the whole body. Emphasis must be placed in all flexible actions on the mobility of the joints and the extension of parts of the body into different areas of the space.

Flexible and fine touch qualities can be combined in gentle weightless stirring, twirling and travelling using rising, spreading and turning and in delicate, undulating interweaving of hands and arms.

Flexible and sudden qualities can be combined in hasty changes of position of hands, in sharp changes of direction, in sudden, lively, "surprise" jumps and turns.

Flexible and sustained qualities can be combined in slow weaving in and out of each other using rising and sinking, twisting and turning in a roundabout, slow-motion manner.

SPACE—LABAN THEMES 3 AND 4

The use of a smaller or larger amount of space will be introduced through the actions of shrinking and expanding, contraction and extension. Rising, subsiding, turning will enable the children to meet with the concept of the levels of high, medium and deep. The natural associations between high and rising and elevation, between medium and turning and spreading and between deep and sinking and beating downward steps can be established. Contrast will be undergone in engaging in actions which remain on or near to one spot and those that cover the whole floor. In general, children of eleven and twelve are still at the stage where they need the opportunity to indulge in the use of as much space as possible. Through their travelling in the space they will become aware of floor pattern in a proper way. Floor pattern will also arise in an uncontrived fashion as a result of relationship tasks and dances. The directions of forwards, backwards and sideways will be used readily.

RELATIONSHIP—LABAN THEME 5

One of the most important relationship situations, particularly for eleven-year-olds who have just transferred to the secondary school, is that of the teacher and the class as a whole. This fosters security in any group from infant children to adults. Simple unison actions such as advancing to the

PLATE 1.—Here we see the first activity of a lesson with a mixed first year C stream class. The aim is to draw the class together and gain a mood of concentration through an advance towards the centre of the group using firm steps. The children are becoming involved but the quality is variable.

PLATE 2.—After repetition, the quality of firmness has improved. The palms of the hands have now become important as a sinking action is used.

PLATE 3.—First year B stream girls are here leaping and travelling with a free choice of body part leading. Some of them are beginning to show a sense of relatedness of body parts in the action.

PLATE 4.—The task for these B stream girls was to make an approach, grip a partner to make a turning jump and leap away again. Differences in hold and in firmness of grip can be observed in the two front pairs; a third pair approach and the fourth are parting.

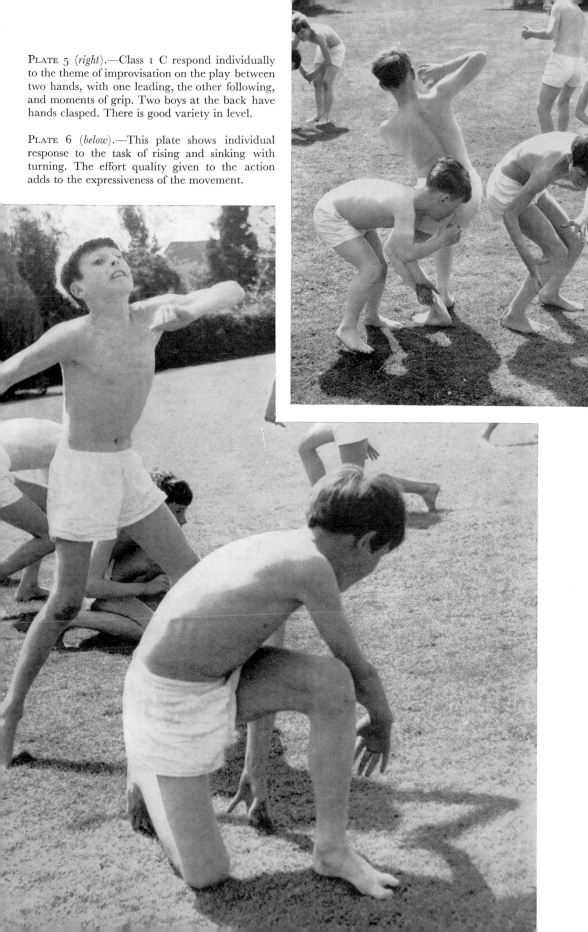

PLATE 5 (*right*).—Class 1 C respond individually to the theme of improvisation on the play between two hands, with one leading, the other following, and moments of grip. Two boys at the back have hands clasped. There is good variety in level.

PLATE 6 (*below*).—This plate shows individual response to the task of rising and sinking with turning. The effort quality given to the action adds to the expressiveness of the movement.

PLATES 7 and 8.—In these two plates we see completely different relationships arising from the same task, that of a simple meeting and parting. In 7 two girls are still approaching as the third leaps between them. In 8 the boys have arrived together in a symmetric group shape.

PLATES 9, 10 and 11.—These illustrations show three contrasting movements from the point of view of body shape, action and relationship of the hands.

PLATES 12–15.—These four illustrations, as also the set shown as plates 16–18 (overleaf), show the children's response to tasks set for groups of three. In each case the task gives a clear framework of action, while scope is left for individual or group interpretation in terms of the part of the body selected to lead the action, the levels and pathways established from the group interplay and the detailed development of the movement phrase.

In this set of four plates we see an approach with a clear emphasis on the body part leading the movement, a mingling of the group and a climax brought about by a lively travelling action.

In plate 12 (*top left*) note the choice of elbow, of finger-tips of one hand and of two hands used to lead in. The girl on the left uses free flow action and therefore approaches with an eagerness to move onwards. The girl on the right shows a contrasting bound flow and therefore looks more ready to stop as she travels inwards.

In plate 13 (*below left*) one girl has passed between the other two and starts to turn alone while the others link together. A gentle action can be observed in the relaxed hands of the single girl.

In plate 14 (*right*) one girl travels between the other two to become the leader.

In plate 15 (*below*) we see the sense of release in the activity of "follow my leader." The girls keep their own style of leaping, however. It is interesting to note the third girl's ease of leaping and to compare this with her earlier use of bound flow in plate 12.

PLATES 16, 17 and 18.—
In this set of three plates
we see another interpre-
tation of the same task.
Here, in plate 16, the
mingling takes place with
linked hands and this
brings about some tension
in their bodies. In plate 17
the leader draws the others
along and in plate 18 they
introduce an ending in
which two break away with
a turning leap, followed by
the leader doing likewise.

PLATES 19–22.—This group meets at different levels with clear lead in the elbows (plate 19, *left*); they continue, in plate 20 (*below*), to change level with elbows and backs leading the spiralling. In plate 21 (*below left*) the first boy leaps away with an oblique jump, while in plate 22 (*below right*) this boy achieves an interesting body shape with a flexed left arm and hand, a stretched right arm and the feet kicked up behind.

PLATES 23–26.—This group meets in a symmetric shape (plate 23, *left*) at high level and with joined hands. Plate 24 (*below*) shows the first girl sinking and turning. Plate 25 (*right*) shows the second starting to turn and plate 26 (*below right*) shows the arrival when the third has turned and joined the others. The qualities of fine touch and sustainment were used throughout, and there is considerable awareness of the relatedness of parts of the body to each other, both individually and with others. Some of the possibilities inherent in the trio relationship are shown clearly here. Thus we see the unison meeting in plate 23 and the idea of moving in turn in plates 24 and 25, while, throughout, the idea of a trio surrounding a central area of the space is important. This little sequence has a unity in its composition since it explores the basic idea of rising to high and sinking to deep, while the turning element is developed between these two levels. The girls do not introduce any irrelevant movement ideas and this, together with their sensitive awareness of each other, makes it a most satisfying sequence.

PLATES 27 and 28.—These two plates show three boys meeting with a firm pressure of their hands. They maintain this as they develop a turning action with sinking. The quality of firmness contrasts with the girls' fine touch in the previous set.

centre of the room and retreating, repeated to establish a rhythm, or travelling around in a linked circle are two examples which are helpful. The scope to work out individual ideas must be considerable since this fulfils the need to make a personal response. It is vital to the future development over subsequent years that confidence in the individual's power to create in movement is established as early as possible. Much emphasis must therefore be placed on the teacher's appreciation of the variety of response shown within a class to a common task. This individual work will be balanced by the chance to work with others. All that belongs to the pair relationship can be explored, and will include meeting and parting, action and reaction, unison and opposition, leading and following.

In developing the idea of response the child could repeat the action of his partner, matching it as nearly as possible. Different actions could be used, as for example, in one leaping while the partner answers with a turning. One could use sudden or light actions while the partner responds with sustained or firm actions. One could rise and spread while the other could close and sink. One could dance using the elbows to lead while the partner could dance using the knees.

In working in unison the pairs could use the same action, at the same time, could work at the same level, lead with the same body part, use the same quality, describe the same shape. Clearly, mirroring and shadowing will be helpful here.

Such possibilities will form the basis of spontaneous improvisation as well as of worked-out sequences which can be memorised. Children will also enjoy working in small groups at this age. Towards the end of the first year progress can be made in work with threes. This asks for a greater awareness and it also gives scope for more variety in pattern and in relationship possibilities. Much of the work at this stage will be better unaccompanied since the emphasis will be upon building personal rhythms. Percussion can, however, be very useful to serve as a stimulus to action and to help to bring about a particular movement quality. The children can handle it sensitively and competently themselves. Its use by a leader or by all members of a group can prove a strong element in establishing rhythm. Also of use as a basis for a short dance are some of the short pieces from the "Listen and Move" series of records.

CHAPTER 6

Second Year Secondary, aged 12–13

THIS is the age at which considerable progress can be made by those with a year's experience behind them. They should have gained movement vocabulary and have been sufficiently encouraged, in lively action and concentration, to have confidence in their abilities. They show considerable independence and will come forward with their own suggestions if there is the appropriate atmosphere for this to happen. There is evidence that they can improvise freely on a theme, retaining concentration for suprisingly long periods. It is, however, worth pointing out that this is more likely to be observed in those children who have already danced in their first year. Those starting dance in the second year need the background which one would normally establish in the first year. Not only can experienced second years become absorbed in improvisation but they can formulate short dances from their exploratory work. They will be prepared to work for long periods of time to clarify and perfect their dances with help from the teacher where needed or asked for. They can watch other pairs or groups with appreciation and can show good powers of observation if constantly encouraged in this.

At this stage, the children's differentiation in terms of movement quality can be very good; they can employ their knowledge of spatial possibilities fully without too much prompting and there is evidence that they are aware, albeit kinaesthetically, of the total sensation inherent in spatial actions. It still remains a challenge for them to bring about clarity in the body, in movement quality and in spatial orientation at one and the same time. This is achieved with practice and it is for this reason that short dances are to be preferred to lengthy, poorly executed ones. There is evidence of enjoyment of varied content from the point of view of mood. Lively, dynamic, rhythmic expression; a more lyrical mood; dramatic interplay: all these are observed in the children's own dance invention. The sense of drama arises particularly from the relationship situations of leading and following, action and reaction, the opposition of different effort qualities and spatial contrasts.

BODY AWARENESS—LABAN THEMES I AND 6

The many aspects mentioned under this heading in the first year scheme will remain important. However, while in the first year these aspects formed the basis of exploration upon which to build a vocabulary, in this year there will be less use of them as the theme upon which a lesson or group of lessons is based. Rather will they remain aspects to be clarified and used appropriately in dances based upon other themes. There is a deeper realisation of the significance of *body shape* in stillness. This is understood and enjoyed both as an individual and as a group expression. An important aspect of progress at this stage is the need to develop the children's ability in using many *parts of the body* in furthering their grasp of effort quality. Having introduced the different qualities through the actions and spatial areas which are most helpful for beginners, the teacher must now encourage the children to use other body parts and areas of space. Unless this exploration happens at this stage, a sterility of expression will result. An example of this which is frequently encountered is that of a pressing action made in an advancing step at a deep level with the palms of the hands leading. The shaping of gestures becomes important during the second year and is further referred to under the heading of "Space" below.

EFFORT—LABAN THEMES 7 AND 8

With movement qualities and their simple combinations now familiar to the children, further progress in this aspect should form a major part of the scheme for this year. The children have the ability to make *transitions between combinations of qualities*. It is a strengthening of this feeling for transition which, together with repetition, brings about rhythm which lays the foundation of dance. The various combinations will give extensive variety. All the possibilities of firmness or fine touch, of suddenness or sustainment, of directness or flexibility, of bound or free flow, can be used. Thus for example the rhythm brought about by the transition from a firm, sustained to a firm, sudden action will be characterised by the time change as the action achieves a speedy ending. As this transition is repeated several times a characteristic rhythm is created. A different action mood would be achieved if the transition was from a firm, sudden to a light, sudden action characterised by the weight change and a decrease in tension. Thus this would bring about a different rhythm from the first example. Yet another example would be the transition from a sustained, direct to a sustained, flexible action characterised by the space change and a pliant ending. The maintenance of sustainment while the spatial element changes produces yet another rhythm. Clearly there is much to be covered under this heading, if the many possible action moods are to be experienced. The compounds of the qualities in the *basic effort actions* should also be included in this year.

BASIC EFFORT ACTIONS: combinations will be made of the qualities of weight, time and space (see page 38). Repetition of these effort actions will bring out their rhythmic nature. Effort transitions will occur in working actions. Experience can be given of different time rhythms and the placing of accent in a phrase.

Thrust: this will be most easily experienced in stepping, jumping and galloping with the accent into the ground and in the use of driving gestures with such parts of the body as fists, elbows, feet and knees. The contrast can be experienced between the final impact of a thrust performed with bound flow and the energy which streams onwards in a free flow thrust.

Dab: this will be most easily experienced by the use of extremities, in light, sudden, precise steps, leaps and jumps, tapping with the feet, in sharp upward movement of the knees, in quick darting out and back with the fingers. This is usually a free flow action but can be bound flow.

Press: this will most easily be experienced in the pressure of one hand against another, in pressure of feet against the floor, in the pressing together and pulling apart of body parts to stress the counter-tension. Pressing is a controlled movement performed with bound flow.

Slash: this will most easily be experienced in the whipping action of arms and legs, the action being of a scattering successive free flow nature. It is helpful to use turning jumps with an asymmetric stress.

Float: this will be most easily experienced in buoyant, weightless stirring and turning, rising and spreading, twisting and weaving in and out of each other with roundabout pathways and plasticity of the body, through the use

SECOND YEARS

PLATE 29 shows the beginning of a lesson in which second year A stream girls are making rising actions using firmness and choosing to stress either one side or both sides of the body. In attempting to preserve the tension as they rise, some difficulty is encountered in the lower half of the body.

PLATE 30.—Here a firm downward action is asked for with a release and recovery through an upward spin. This is clearly easier to achieve than the previous task.

PLATE 31.—The firm upward pressure is attempted again in a phrase which gives a rhythm through a spin downwards. The fact that each girl developed her own rhythm is shown by the varying positions in which they have been caught.

In the following plates we see two different interpretations of the same task. We see air pattern and floor pattern emerging from the interplay of individuals within small groups. We also see their sense of drama arising from relationship situations.

PLATES 32–35.—In these plates we see the interplay of two trios.

In plate 32 (*left*) the two groups arrive at close quarters; in plate 33 (*below*) the two leaders make contact while the others surround them. This resolves so that the trios re-form and in plate 34 (*right*) one group drives the other back. Finally a driving action of those who previously retreated causes a reversal. The focus of the one group remains outward while the others sink down and close away, as seen in the final plate.

PLATES 36, 37 and 38.—The centre of the space between these girls is obviously important as a focus for meeting and from which to spring away. Clarity in the use of the body in changes of level and in qualities of sustainment and suddenness can be observed.

of many directions for the joints and body parts. The contrast can be experienced between the more guided movement as performed with bound flow and the greater fluency in free flow.

Wring: this will be most easily experienced in strong turning and twisting with tension in the body and the use of downward directions, bound flow and counter-tension.

Flick: this will be most easily experienced in fingers and wrists moving in a quick, lively, roundabout way, in light turns and leaps and scattering gestures, using free flow.

Glide: this will be most easily experienced in smoothing gestures using palms and marking clear, straight, bound flow pathways through the space, in rising upwards and in stepping, although this is more difficult because of balance.

It will be seen that while in the first year the main stress is upon the achievement of a wide vocabulary of body awareness and simple quality and spatial awareness, this year sees the main area of progress in the realm of effort. This is because of the importance of stressing the relationship between inner impulse and outer effort at an age when the children are becoming aware in a more conscious way of their individuality. Moreover, this experience of the rhythmical content, so vital to dance and arising from the bodily action must be given at this stage. As Laban wrote in *Modern Educational Dance:*

> "Dancing-plays of the higher age groups will approach more and more what we are accustomed to consider as dance compositions."

SPACE—LABAN THEME 9

As already indicated progress is made during this year from simple spatial ideas to more advanced ones. The use of different levels comes without prompting and it has been noted that if rostra are in the hall used for dance, these prove a strong attraction to this age group as a means of emphasising height and depth.

Progress lies in the field of pattern. The awareness of pattern comes from gesture, in which the active part of the body may lead from the centre of the body outwards, from the periphery into the centre; may traverse the space from one place on the periphery to another; may wrap around the body; may vary in extension. The pattern then is established from clear action and the children will be able to observe the patterns made by each other. Patterns will vary in size, in direction and in level. They may be symmetric or asymmetric in shape. The difference in expression between angular, curved and twisted patterns will be recognised. While air pattern comes fundamentally from the inner impulse leading into space and so evolving a form, floor pattern arises basically from the enlargement of movement so that the general space of the room is entered. Thus the freely flowing movement of the children brings with it floor pattern. Perhaps the most important way in which floor pattern arises is through the interplay with others. In mixed classes of this age group it seems that girls will tend to stress the pattern in their creative work while the boys lay greater stress on the action and quality.

Awareness of body shape is particularly evident in the ending of a phrase of movement and the children will be able to observe the more one-dimensional, penetration of an "arrow-like" shape which might arise from, say, a piercing upward thrust; the two-dimensional "wall-like" shape that might be produced, for example, from a broad spreading movement; the three-dimensional "ball-like" shape arrived at from a closing, sinking turn, or the three-dimensional "screw-like" shape which might be the culmination of a turning and twisting action.

RELATIONSHIP—LABAN THEME 5

At this age the pair relationship is still enjoyed, as are small groups in simple situations, but there is now increased sensitivity in working in threes. Three is a good number in creative situations as everyone can be involved and can readily make a contribution. In establishing the possibilities in trios the pupils should become aware of the fact that with this number they can establish a small group and a circle, possibilities not present in a partner relationship. The movements of shrinking and spreading, of swaying to and fro, of rising to meet in the centre and spreading out and sinking on the edge, or viceversa, of circling with a rhythmical stepping or a spinning action, are all to be explored. The short line that a three can make holds possibilities of swaying to and fro or of the pull upon the centre person which can be exerted from either end. The line can make a tiny spiral, the leader can travel through an arch made by the other two. New possibilities exist, not contained in the duo, of one passing between two to split them or to link them; the middle person can be swung to and fro; an interweaving can take place in which figure-of-eight pathways will be traced. In working out the relationships inherent in the trio, there is clearly scope for the individual to dance alone, for one to relate to two and for the three to work in unison. The idea of a canon form can also be used as can the possibilities of high, medium and deep levels.

Although older primary school children will use and enjoy the possibilities of the interaction of threes, twelve-year-olds are able to react to this challenge in a more conscious manner. They show the ability to stand back, as it were, from their improvisations, to recognise the moments of unison, of individual action, of action and reaction and to be able to clarify the forms that emerge from their "dance plays."

CHAPTER 7

Third Year Secondary, aged 13–14

THIS is an interesting and challenging age group to work with in dance. Girls of this age are growing physically and are looking mature. Despite this there is often a certain instability as adjustments are being made. There is a need for encouragement and praise to preserve confidence and a strong desire is shown to be involved in the group, and not to be left out. This desire to make a personal contribution may express itself through discussion and argument about the work in hand, as well as through participation in the dance itself. It has been observed that a class who would previously have been content to get on with group tasks with a minimum of talking became more talkative about their dances at this stage. As one experienced teacher put it, the motto for the year is: "Possess your soul in patience."

Allowing for all that has been said above and in Chapter 3 about problems with the third year, for those progressing on a sound foundation of experience in the previous two years this can be a remarkable and rewarding year. The pupils have the ability to bring about the integration of bodily activity, effort quality and spatial awareness. They are confident in the knowledge already gained. Not only have they a movement vocabulary but they can observe well and have gained a terminology which is meaningful, being based on experience. They now know what is expected of them by the teacher in terms of individual participation. They have gained a sense of achievement from the opportunities which have been presented to them of working with others in a creative situation.

During the third year they are able to concentrate for longer periods on a piece of work and they can sustain interest and memory over several weeks, being able to regain quality more quickly after a week's gap. They will readily bring music and suggest themes which they would like to use. In this year we see the inclusion of the advanced themes 10–13.

BODY AWARENESS—LABAN THEMES 1, 6, 12 AND 13

At this stage progress can be made in the aspect of labile equilibrium. The theme of *elevation* demands more than the ability to leave the ground. Even though many girls of this age are getting heavier—perhaps because of this—it seems important to develop the pupils' capacity for elevation. While heavier children may find difficulty in lifting their weight far from the ground, those who remain slight in build will perform this with ease. In leaving the ground a great clarity can be expected from the point of view of the rhythmical content, as mentioned in connection with the five basic jumps covered in the syllabus for the 11–12 age group. The height of the jump, the slope of the body in flight, the degree of turn if this is involved and the overall fluency: all these can be clarified. Moreover, at this stage of development, the expression in a rising action has a real feeling for the sensation of elevation. This is seen in the movement of those not able to achieve great height. Mastery of this theme enhances the feeling for dance which should be emerging strongly in the third year. As Laban wrote in *Modern Educational Dance*:

> "Of all body functions skips, leaps and jumps are the most characteristic dancing actions because they can constitute the main effort of a whole dance."

There is also increased ability in the use of different *body parts* in performing efforts and in shaping gestures with a good sense of integration of the body as a whole being evident.

EFFORT—LABAN THEMES 10 AND 12

The emphasis on themes concerned with the *combinations of the eight basic effort actions* in Theme 10 stresses the importance of the total involvement in bodily action and gives scope for, indeed encourages, the concentration so necessary for this age group. There is a wealth of material here in exploring the weight, time and space rhythms, and in extending the work started in the second year. Here is derived the stuff of the rhythmical dynamic aspect of dance, not from external musical rhythms, but from the quality changes in effort transitions.

Experience should be given in all the rhythmical variations. If we start with the basic effort action of *thrust*, in which all the fighting elements of firmness, suddenness and directness are present, a change in one of these elements will bring about a transition to another effort. The combination of these two efforts in a phrase will have its own distinctive rhythm. The following possibilities occur.

In *thrust–dab* we have a weight rhythm and this could be experienced by a stepping action in which sharp accented steps alternated with light steps. Inward thrusting elbows, alternating with upward dabbing in finger-tips, would aid the expression. In *thrust–press* we have a time rhythm and this could be experienced by a thrust of the elbow leading into a pressing gesture with the forearm, together with stepping. In *thrust–slash* we have a space rhythm and this could be experienced by an inward thrust of one elbow followed by an outward slashing turning jump led by the other arm.

Similar rhythmical developments can be made by taking as a basis the effort action of *floating* in which the indulging elements of fine touch, sustainment and flexibility are present. The following possibilities occur.

In *float–wring* we have a weight rhythm and this could be experienced in a rising, turning action of the whole body led by the hands followed by a sinking, twisting, screwing action led by the elbows. In *float–flick* we have a time rhythm and this could be experienced in a floating gesture of the arms and free leg which quickens into a sudden gesture of the hands and feet.

In *float–glide* we have a space rhythm and this could be experienced in a light flexible, sustained leg gesture followed by a direct gliding action in the arm, together with stepping. Other weight rhythms are *press–glide* which could be experienced in a gesture, accompanied by steps, which starts at a deep level and gradually rises and sinks to repeat again, and *slash–flick* which could be experienced in flexible, turning jumps which alternate energetic slashes with light, delicate flicks.

Other time rhythms are *dab–glide* which could be experienced in a sudden action in the finger-tips leading to a smoothing gesture, and *slash–wring* which could be experienced in a turn which starts with a sudden impulsive burst of energy and decelerates into a firm, flexible, deep screwing action.

Other space rhythms are *dab–flick* which could be experienced through light jumps and hand gestures in which direct pin-pointing alternates with flexibility, and *press–wring* which could be experienced in downward pressure of the lower half of the body followed by flexibility in the upper half.

Such effort-transitions can quite clearly also be performed in the opposite order to that already given—for example *dab–thrust* or *flick–float* or *wring–press*. This again makes for a new expression. Different parts of the body can be used for the different parts of the rhythm. Repetition must be used to establish the particular rhythm; the motif can be developed in size; locomotion and elevation can be used and this will in turn create pathways in the space. Groups working in this way may find themselves using voice sound or percussion to emphasise the particular dynamics.

An exciting aspect is the interplay of groups each using their own rhythms and possibly influencing each other or arriving at a common rhythm which incorporates their various group rhythms. Thus, for example, three groups could take the transitions related to thrusting. Each group could first of all establish their rhythm in unison on the spot; a development could take place whereby a relationship could be established with the other groups; the rhythmical motifs could be developed in size using travelling, elevation and turning so that approaches are made towards the other groups. For example such rhythms as these could be used:

Thrust–dab–dab, Thrust–dab–dab, Thrust–dab–dab, Thrust–thrust–
  thrust
Press–thrust, Press–thrust, Press–thrust, Press—
Slash–thrust–thrust, Slash–thrust–thrust, Slash–thrust–thrust, Slash–
  slash

On meeting, each group could in turn state their rhythm to which the others react and the sequence might finish with a shared thrusting action.

A contrasting mood can be created through using the transitions related to *floating*. Thus, the weight rhythm group, *thrust–dab*, might use as a contrast the *float–wring* combination, the time rhythm group, *thrust–press*, might use as a contrast the *float–flick* combination and the space rhythm group, *thrust–slash*, might use the *float–glide* combination.

Given scope to experiment the pupils will use all manner of step patterns, elevation and gesture and will gain rich experience in the language of movement.

Such work can be extended further by using the transitions between several effort actions, for example *press–glide–float* in which the weight change gives way to a space change or *thrust–slash–wring* in which the space change gives way to a time change.

Alternating with sequences and dance plays where the rhythms come directly from the movement, dances can be formulated in which music of a dynamic nature is the starting-point. In this case "pure" effort actions will probably not occur but variations of tension, of forte and pianissimo, of sudden staccato or sustained legato passages, of lines of melody that lead directly along or rise and sink in a more flexible fashion, will act as a stimulus to invention.

The tendency is for teachers to fall back entirely upon music and dramatic ideas so that the quite different personal rhythms arising from the use of effort transitions is rarely experienced. Effort rhythms are often used solely as material for imposed studies rather than as a basis for movement motifs and dance. Thus their full potential is not explored.

SPACE—LABAN THEMES 11 AND 12

An understanding of the close link between effort and space will be established through the work in effort. It will become evident that the action may penetrate the space directly or may use it in a flexible and wavy fashion. The size of the action may vary and different levels and areas will be used; the repetition of a rhythm may bring about extension in the space and cause subsequent floor pattern and interplay with other groups.

At this stage the movement possibilities inherent in the concept of the two-dimensional planes can be introduced and with their stable and less mobile expression can serve a useful purpose at an age when stable expression with its secure balance can be helpful to the pupils. Clearly the emphasis must always remain on the spatial action rather than on the arrival at points of orientation.

Movement in the *door plane* will give an experience of the circling action which involves rising, opening, sinking, crossing. Thus the shaping in the plane brings about a restriction in the crossing, freedom in the opening, firmness in the downward and fine touch in the upward development of the form. An appreciation should be gained of the barrier-like extension

64

THIRD YEARS

This third year B stream class are at the beginning of their second term and are working on basic effort actions and effort rhythms.

PLATE 39 (*right*).—In this plate we see the moment when the girls meet, having travelled with flicking jumps. The two front girls have kept the fine touch in legs as well as hands. The two on the outside are still weighty in hips and shoulders.

PLATE 40 (*below*).—Here the girls attempt to follow a flicking meeting with a dabbing retreat. Several of them achieve the fine touch and suddenness but the girl at the back brings in firmness in shoulder and hand.

PLATE 41.—The second half of a sequence in which thrusting steps forward were followed by a slashing jump back to the starting-place. In their movement we can observe their ability to exert energy to drive themselves upwards and backwards. Their flying hair indicates their sudden attitude to time. They also show that they are beginning to be able to use flexibility in combination with the firmness and suddenness. Their bodies fill the space as they describe three-dimensional forms and create round-about pathways. With more experience they will be able to bring out the flexibility through using the curving, arching and twisting possibilities in the trunk.

PLATE 42.—The task here was to advance with thrusting leaps. It is interesting to note that the sudden energetic attack is present and that sharp parts of the body are used to lead the movement. Thus we see the elbows and the knees used, while one of the girls uses the forearm and another leads with the whole arm and hand, her back leg stressing the counter direction. Of special interest is the fact that the forward travelling action has encouraged free flow which tends to replace the directness for some girls.

PLATE 43 (*above*).—Response to the task of meeting with a dabbing action has created a lighthearted mood.

PLATE 44 (*left*).—The meeting is followed by a sudden parting with the emphasis on lively fingers and feet. The two front girls preserve a fine touch quality in this action.

PLATES 45 and 46.—In these plates two situations are captured which occur within the many possibilities of two trios working in relationship with each other. The shape created by the linked group, which is building a unison rising and sinking motif, provides a spatial stimulus for the other trio. They respond to this by surrounding and by weaving through the spaces. The closed group preserves its shape while the line adapts in a more mobile way, using changes of level. In this way, air and floor patterns are created from the group interplay.

PLATE 47.—The task here was that of a group advance with thrusting actions led by the elbow. The firmness is clearly evident in the legs, arms and backs of the leader and the girl to the right of her.

PLATE 48.—In contrasting mood the group weave through each other as they make a transition from the direct, sudden firm action to a flexible, sustained fine touch action. The fine touch is just beginning to be achieved by some girls.

The following sequence of plates captures moments of group action and of interplay in the dance drama freely based on the story of "Theseus," described on page 69. This B stream class started dance in their second year.

PLATES 49 and 50.—In the two plates on this page a group use a firm action in knees and fists as they meet and part with rising and sinking. Through this group movement a sense of unity is established.

PLATES 51 and 52 (*facing page*).—The leader draws her group through a barrier, the to-and-fro pull growing in size until a break occurs.

PLATE 53 (*above*).—Here a group formed a closely knit barrier through which the leader broke by splitting apart first the front pair and later, after they had rejoined, the second pair. She used actual touch to achieve the breakthrough and her movement was a thrusting action of both arms and one leg. These group barriers when penetrated re-formed into a spiral pathway along which the leader travelled to the centre of the maze.

PLATE 54 (*left*).—Having reached the centre of the spiral, the leader brings out her dominance through the contrast between her firm rising action and the collapse of the group through which she has travelled. The use of the dais helps to accentuate the difference in level.

in which the body, with the upright spine and lateral bend, separates the area in front from that behind. An experience should be given of the stable stance which emphasises the "present" state where neither step nor gesture indicates advance or retreat. Dance plays within the plane will involve stepping sideways, rising and sinking and elevation. Scope is present for the face-to-face relationship with a partner, or between two groups, which may be of a confronting or of a sensitive mirroring nature.

Movement in the *wheel plane* will give an experience of the circling action which involves advancing, sinking, retreating, rising. Thus the shaping in the plane brings about a rhythmical expression caused by the alternation of advance and retreat together with the firmness associated with sinking and the fine touch associated with rising. An appreciation should be gained of curving and arching of the spine, with the use of the limbs, which is involved in the wave-like action, in which the body separates the area to the right side from that on the left without any sideways deviation. An experience should be given of the progression and withdrawal with the characteristic bowing and uprising typical of movement in this plane. Dance plays within the plane will involve stepping with advance and retreat, elevation and arm and leg gesture. Scope is present for the relationship situation of meeting and parting and of action and reaction and of interplay using successive bodily action of a mobile nature.

Movement in the *table plane* will include the circling action which involves opening, advancing, crossing, retreating. Thus the shaping in the plane brings about an alert awareness associated with the restriction of the crossing, the freedom of the opening together with the progression and withdrawal. An appreciation should be gained of the spreading of the movement at medium level with twisting in the spine, which separates the area above from that below with neither rise nor sink. Dance plays in this plane will involve stepping in circular pathways and the use of turns and gesture, with the characteristic calming, smoothing nature. Scope is present for the relationship situations of surrounding, approaching, retreating, leading and following on curved paths, and for the interplay of curving patterns in which meeting, parting, passing, travelling together and using a common centre for a group may occur.

The intersection of these planes with each other can make points of transition from movement in one plane to that in another. In this way dance forms may be created in which the interplay of movement in the three planes can be explored. The symbolic expression of adoration and admiration associated with rising in the door plane, the expression of blessing associated with advancing in the table plane, the expression of bowing and reverence associated with sinking in the wheel plane have formed the basis of many dances which convey an overall mood of praise or worship.

RELATIONSHIP—LABAN THEME 6

At this stage there is considerable enjoyment in working in larger groups, in establishing relationship and in clarifying the relationship content within their dance experiences. The pupils still enjoy the pair and trio situations. They now have the concentration which enables them to build up dances in which several different relationships occur. Thus they may start alone, approach another and dance with them, travel to join other pairs and form small groups, and finally pursue the possibility of relating all groups to each other through, say, an approach to meet in the centre of the room.

Whether in the realm of body awareness and action, as for example, in elevation, or in the realm of effort as, for example, in the many rhythmical possibilities introduced earlier in this chapter, or in the realm of space as, for example, in the shaping of the planes, it is important that the individual exercises, improvisations and motifs culminate in shared activity. In this way the movement experience will develop into dance.

There are two principal ways in which the development of group motifs can be brought about. On the one hand the class can work to master their individual inventions and create personal dance motifs. A small group can then attempt to master a chosen individual motif. This enables the teacher to pick out an unusual motif which may provide a challenge to a group. It also makes sure that those not normally taking a lead, or those who may be less popular as leaders, may be given this opportunity. The very fact of the teacher selecting a motif created by a pupil, not usually recognised as a leader or as particularly gifted, may help to establish the pupil in a more positive role in the group. It also serves to encourage the more passive members of the class who may otherwise regularly rely on the inventions of others in the group. It goes without saying that it is important that at some stage or other all the pupils are put into the position of having their motifs selected.

When this method of arriving at a group motif is employed, it is important that time is given for the motif to be completely mastered so that everyone in the group feels confident in its performance. Three illustrations of tasks which could lend themselves to this treatment are given here as examples. An action task could ask for leaping or hopping and travelling to establish an individual rhythm. An effort task could ask for thrusting steps alternating with light, precise jumps or skips to establish an individual sequence. A spatial task could ask for circling arm and leg gestures in the wheel plane using increase and decrease of size with advancing and retreating. The group may follow the individual whose motif has been selected as a loosely formed unit or as a line. It should be borne in mind that although children enjoy the play situation of "follow my leader" which occurs in the line, too long a line or too complicated a motif will not make for mastery by everyone. The small group, fairly close to the leader, stands a better chance of mastering the motif as a unison experience.

The second method by which a group motif may be achieved is through starting as a group with a common task. Ideally, in this situation, the tasks should be selected so that they lend themselves to a shared response. Three illustrations of tasks which could be suitable for this treatment are given here. An action task could ask for a linked circle to travel around the centre with a stepping rhythm which culminates in a downward accented jump, on both feet, the phrase being repeated in either the same or the opposite direction. An effort task could ask for a group to approach the centre of their circle using a pressing action to meet, a gliding action to rise and to part with a turning, floating action. A spatial task could ask for a group facing in a common direction to rise with sudden light repeated movements and to spread, open and sink with symmetric arm gestures.

Clearly the establishment of group motifs is only a beginning. From such beginnings developments of motifs will occur and can be encouraged by the teacher. From the repetition of the motif as it stands the rhythm will become clear. When this has been established the motif may be diminished in size or increased in size. The latter will bring about travelling and turning and possibly elevation. The important moments of climax within such a developed motif must be discovered and emphasised, as must be a clear beginning and ending. At this stage we begin to see the development of simple dance forms, as one motif and development is possibly contrasted by a second motif, or as the original motif is varied through the use of a different quality. Examples taken from the earlier suggestions in this section may serve to illustrate the point. If the motif (a) was based on the wheel plane it could be performed originally with only one or two steps of advance or retreat. The development of (a) could involve increase in size and emphasis on the advance so that the group travel through the space arriving in a new place in the room, halting in a forward direction. A contrasting motif (b) could be created using a turning, spreading action in the table plane and eventually establishing a front facing towards the original starting-place. The travelling development of (a) could be repeated back to the starting-place and finally (a) itself could be repeated in its original rhythm.

To take another example, if the motif (a) was based on a centrally facing group who approached with a pressing action, rose with a glide and separated with a turning float, motif (b) could be concerned with the pressing element and might be taken in a pathway which approached and then surrounded the centre of the group, separating again at the end. This could be followed by (a). Motif (c) could be concerned with rising, gliding, travelling around the periphery of the circle. Once more (a) could be repeated. Motif (d) could be concerned with a mingling using the floating action to fill the space previously used by the inner pressing circle or the outer gliding one. Finally, (a) could be repeated once more. This clearly brings about a rondo form.

Such pieces of work which form the basis of dance composition may be performed to music to provide a rhythmical or melodic framework suitable for the movement theme on which the teacher is working. However, music is not essential as the rhythms can come from the movement itself, or voice accompaniment or percussion could be added as the final stage.

In addition to the two methods enlarged upon above, group relationships may be developed from a group following the improvised movements of a leader. This is a more spontaneous activity and calls for imagination on the part of the leader and quick response from the group. It has its place, however, as it is often from improvisation and spontaneous dance play that new movement ideas are discovered.

The group dances and dance dramas which the teacher may work out with the group can be successful only if the pupils have had opportunities to work on short group motifs. Whatever the theme, it has to be transmuted into the language of movement, either by the teacher or the class, as they gain experience.

The theme of "Theseus" taken with a third year group after two years of dance had the following "story." The victims, whose turn it is to travel to Minos to be sacrificed to the Minotaur, part from or are expelled by the people. Theseus appears as the leader of this band. With the help of a skein of thread Theseus finds his way out of the labyrinth and escapes with the other victims.

The movement content was concerned with group motifs to stress unity, the separation or expulsion of individuals from each group, the forming of a new group by those expelled, the establishment of a strong leader, the leading of this group through other groups who formed a series of barriers reminiscent of a labyrinth and the final victorious emergence.

Within such a theme scope exists for clarity of effort quality and spatial form in the group relationship.

Finally, as Laban wrote in his notes on the advanced themes:

"The movement drama can be a story of tragic or comic content, but the conflict and solution of movement contrast are in themselves a dramatic affair, needing no excuse in a story, which might be built up around them. In the same way, lyricism in dance is not, say, a description of events in nature or feeling, but a performance of movement sequences in which dramatically conflicting contrasts and their solution recede into the background."

CHAPTER 8

Fourth Year Secondary, aged 14–15

FOR those developing the work further with fourth years who have three years of background, this is a time of great progress. In this year the pupils settle down after any restlessness associated with the third year, and the teacher reaps the benefit of the hard work of earlier years.

The interest exhibited in the third year through the bringing of music and the suggestion of themes is sustained. There is also an indication that pupils will ask if they themselves may work out their ideas with the whole class.

The emphasis is upon group relationships and dance forms so that the earlier material of body awareness, effort and space is used within the dance experiences. It must be borne in mind that although sensitivity in group feeling grows with maturity and is a theme to be continued with fifth and sixth form pupils, a start should be made in this year.

For a few years, before the raising of the school leaving age to 16, some fourth years will be in their final year. For these pupils it is important that the emphasis is firmly placed on the themes concerned with relationship and dance and dance drama experience. For those remaining at school for one or more years fresh study aspects in the areas of effort and space can be introduced as well as the work in relationship.

BODY AWARENESS—LABAN THEMES I, 12 AND 13.

Developments in this aspect are concerned with the work in effort and space. In connection with effort (Theme 12) the possibilities of executing efforts with different body parts, as well as those used most readily, are to be pursued.

A further progression is in performing an effort or in shaping a movement with different body parts taking over during the pattern. Moreover, several body parts can be brought into play at the same time.

The elevation introduced in the previous year will continue to be important since leaping and jumping constitute a major element in dance. Confidence in managing the body in flight is gained at this stage.

EFFORT—LABAN THEMES 10 AND 12

The work on effort rhythms begun in the previous year will be continued in the fourth year. As mastery is gained in the combinations of basic effort actions (Theme 10), the themes concerned with the performance of shapes and efforts by different parts of the body (Theme 12) can be further pursued. As indicated in the sections on effort covered in the syllabus for years 1 and 2, certain qualities of movement are more easily experienced when entering relevant areas of space and when using particular parts of the body. Thus, for example, fine touch will be experienced more readily in a rising action with emphasis on the lift of the breast bone, while firmness will be best experienced through a sinking action with emphasis on the lowering of the hips. Similarly, sustainment will readily be experienced through a gesture led by the hands out into the area stretching in front, while suddenness will be best experienced through the hasty inward and backward recoil in the centre of the body. Flexibility will readily be experienced through the plasticity of an opening and spreading action in which the arms, legs and torso can enter the space on the open side of the body, while directness is best experienced through the restricted linear use of the limbs as they pass across the body to their opposite sides. This correlation of simple quality and spatial area makes for harmonious action and forms the basis of the correlation between the diagonal directions and the eight basic effort actions. Less harmonious correlations of effort and spatial direction should be included to give a contrasting experience.

In using different parts of the body for the performance of a particular effort, group interplay can take place. For example, within one group individuals could exert a pressing–gliding rhythm by employing different body parts to lead. For instance, one may use a foot, another a hand, a third a shoulder, a fourth the back and a fifth an elbow. This makes for a different group experience from that in which everyone uses the same part of the body into the same direction. Moreover, as stated in the syllabus for year 3, different body parts can be used for different sections of the pattern.

In observing a phrase of efforts the pattern formed in the space can be noted. The direct efforts will naturally enough tend to produce straight lines, angular pathways or a stretch on a broad curve, while the flexible efforts will produce curves, spirals and twisted forms. For example, a phrase of press–glide–float–flick–slash might develop a form in which the straight path of the press taken into a crossed downward direction would form an angle with the rising line of the glide; this in turn would curve and undulate in an opening float and accelerate in small circles for the flicking with a final twist of a slashing turn.

With the enlargement of the form to introduce steps and the repetition of efforts, floor pattern arises.

For detailed exposition of this aspect readers are recommended to study *Handbook for Modern Educational Dance* and *Choreutics*.

SPACE—LABAN THEMES 11 AND 12

In addition to the work already referred to under the heading of EFFORT, further progress can be made in connection with space orientation (Theme 11). Where the pupils have a good grasp of simple dimensions and of the planes, and the teacher is confident of the advanced material, further possibilities can be introduced. Based on the experiences of circuits in the three planes, discussed in detail in the syllabus for year 3, developments can take place in developing the pupils' understanding of the orientation in the planes.

If the lifting and lowering in the high–deep dimension is given an added expression through the opening or crossing of the right and left sides of the body, then the points of orientation arrived at will be high-right, high-left, deep-right, deep-left.

If the advancing and retreating in the forward–backward dimension is given an added expression through the rising or lowering of the body, then the points of orientation arrived at will be forward-high, forward-deep, backward-high, backward-deep.

If the opening and crossing in the right–left dimension is given an added expression through the advancing or retreating of the body, then the points of orientation arrived at will be right-forward, right-backward, left-forward, left-backward.

72

FOURTH YEARS

This group of A stream girls started dance in their second year and had dance lessons alternating with gymnastics in their third year. These photographs were taken at the beginning of the second term of the fourth year.

PLATES 55 and 56.—These girls are beginning to work on effort rhythms, the purpose being to establish the fundamental idea that rhythm is derived from the changes in effort used by the mover. The girls had worked individually to establish the rhythm derived from the change of weight brought about in making a transition from a pressing to a gliding action. The girls were then asked to work in small groups to create a group action in which not only was the unison press-glide rhythm to be established, but also the arm gesture, step pattern and pathway were to be in unison. Clearly this type of task asks for increased mastery in bodily action. It calls for a sensitive awareness of the other members of the group, and the ability to observe clearly. In plate 55 the girl at the back is obviously watching the leader carefully. In plate 56 the general form has been established, but details such as the turn of the hand still need clarification.

PLATE 57 (*above*).—This class is still working on effort rhythms. Here the task was to use any part of the body, other than hands, to lead a pressing action.

PLATE 58 (*left*).—In this improvisation, in which group sensitivity is the main theme, a group of six has subdivided into two small circles and continued to bring out harmony.

The final set of plates come into a slightly different category as the girls are in costume. All of the class took part in this dance which was worked out for the Christmas Service. The music was from Poulenc's "Gloria" and the motifs were based on the three planes. The girls themselves asked if they could make costumes, sent for samples of material, asked the Needlework mistress to help with the pattern and made their own dresses.

PLATE 59.—The motifs in the wheel plane are used to symbolise the idea of adoration and worship because of the forward, upward reaching, shown clearly by the girl at the front, and because of the development of the motif into the forward deep bowing action. While the common intention is brought out through the unison movement, scope remains for the individual variants. The movement quality is that of an impulsive surging forward in the wheel plane.

PLATE 60.—Another group uses motifs in the table plane to symbolise the idea of benediction. This motif uses arm gestures which spread at medium level and are developed in the dance into turning and travelling. The movement quality is of a gentle smoothing character and contrasts with the more lively action of the previous group.

PLATE 61 (*left*).—This girl brings out clearly the sense of forward progression with the lift of head and arms characteristic of the advancing and rising gesture which occurs in the wheel plane.

PLATE 62 (*below*).—In this plate all the groups join in a final rising in the door plane.

Clearly possibilities now occur of linking these points of orientation. Such links will travel across the kinesphere neither passing through the centre nor keeping on the periphery. Movements along these inclinations have their own particular expression. They have neither the stability of the dimensions nor the extreme lability of the diagonals, but in them the diagonal pull is deflected by a dimensional stress. These transversals are more naturally used by the body than either the pure dimension or pure diagonal. Contained within them we find the interplay between the factors which control human movement—the uprightness of the spine, the right–left symmetry of the body and the forward and backward bending of the spine essential for action.

Movements starting in the high–deep (door) plane and transversing the space to the forward–backward (wheel) plane have, because of their mainly dropping or uprising character, a steep nature. Movements starting in the right–left (table) plane and transversing the space to the high–deep (door) plane have, because of their mainly opening or crossing character, a flat nature. Movements starting in the forward–backward (wheel) plane and transversing the space to the right–left (table) plane have, because of their mainly advancing and retreating character, a flowing nature.

Pupils with, it must be reiterated, a good background can be led to experience these new expressions, and to use them as the basis for dance motifs. It is worth stressing that there is no great virtue in the pupils knowing a series of scales such as the dimensional or the diagonal scales, or in their having a knowledge of all the steep, flat and flowing inclinations. Far more important is the use of this material as a basis for group inventions and dances. To establish the point further, just one idea, out of a wealth of material, is given here. If preliminary individual experience had taken place in connection with the steep inclinations, the material could be explored in a pair or a quartet relationship. Such movements could be included as: from a symmetric open high position with arms reaching high-right and high-left, drop with an advance to bring both hands to meet in forward-deep and thus to meet the other(s), rise tracing the dimension to arrive at forward-high, lift and spread to the starting situation; with the right side trace this inclination and follow with the left side; from the forward-deep point of arrival an opening and retreating could bring an arrival at

G

deep-right and deep-left and from this situation an uprising could take place with either an advance or retreat and consequent new relationship possibilities; the size of the movement could be varied and thus bring about stepping. Throughout such inventions the emphasis must be on the movements themselves—the uprising or dropping, the advancing or retreating of the main movements, with the transitions given similar clarity in bodily action—rather than linking points around the body.

The three-ring trace forms with which some teachers may be familiar establish a particular rhythm as they link steep, flat and flowing inclinations in one phrase of movement. They too can form the basis of invention and interplay—of unison expression, of canon form, of travelling and turning as the form is enlarged and locomotion takes place.

It is assumed that such material as this will be introduced only by teachers who are in full mastery of it, through their own practical experience as well as through a theoretical knowledge of space harmony. The basis of space harmony, and indeed of harmony of movement in general, is set out in great detail in the book *Choreutics*, which is essential study material for any teacher embarking on advanced space work. Criticisms of older pupils being given directed studies and dances where they are "poking into the space" are not without foundation. Until the teacher has acquired a real understanding of the principles underlying this work, it is much wiser to concentrate on other important aspects.

RELATIONSHIP—LABAN THEME 14

A distinction must be drawn between the interplay brought out in partner relationships, trios and groups already discussed in the previous chapter, and the sensitivity required in the awakening of group feeling (Theme 14).

Dances and dance dramas coming into the first category will still be important and the possibilities inherent in the pair and trio relationships will still be enjoyed and will provide a less demanding relationship situation. Nevertheless sensitivity to others in a group should be encouraged. Small groups of five provide a good number, large enough to constitute a group and yet not so large as to make contact between members difficult.

The simplest way of awakening this sensitivity to others is through unison rising and sinking in a free grouping or a simple circle. In this activity the problem of balance in stepping is eliminated. A light touch will help to unify the group. In first attempts, it is important that everyone can see someone else in the group as this increases the possibility of working in unison. The introduction of a change of quality from a firmer sinking to a gentler rising will help to establish a rhythm which in itself heightens unity. Other actions which help to achieve group unity, and do not involve stepping, are swaying to and fro and a circling motion involving knees, hips, spine and head.

The task of approaching to touch lightly, separating again in unison so that all arrive at the same moment in proximity and at a distance, requires sensitive participation, and practice. Variations of time, as in a sustained meeting and sudden parting, will emphasise the rhythmical unity and demand individual mastery in order to achieve group unity.

Still more difficult is the task of a group circling as a body. This can of course be further complicated by the addition of rising and sinking and even expansion and contraction of the group. Increase in speed brings about the exuberance of a whirling, spinning action.

A group can spread from the centre not only in a symmetric way but also with a stress towards a particular direction.

On the basis of unison group action which remains in a relatively small area, progress can be made to group travelling into the space of the room. If a light touch is maintained the group can take varied pathways with changes of direction, can wheel or spin, can rise or sink. Changes of mood will arise from the dynamic changes of energetic or gentle and speedy and sustained variants as well as from the different pathways traced. In such group action a leader will inevitably emerge. With a small group of five or six there is ample opportunity for everyone to take a turn at leading the group so that this responsibility or pleasure is available to all. Further problems occur if the group shape is that of a line rather than a more compact unit. Joining in some way or other may help to emphasise the link between the individuals. Much is required of the leader if the sense of unity is to be brought about. Indeed adults find this a challenge.

It is helpful to set a task which is concerned with the use of the space and the interplay with other line groups in the class so that streaming across the room—encircling another group, spiralling and unwinding—stresses the scope of the line. What is less helpful is individual personal action and especially turning on one's own axis—an activity which if employed by the leader, and followed in turn down the line, destroys the unity of the line. This sort of group awareness in a line is quite different from a follow-my-leader play in which the leaping or stepping action is predominantly important and any sense of group unity comes from the common action rather than sensitive co-operation in a shared situation.

Clearly groups or lines travelling about the space leads inevitably to the interplay of groups. At an earlier stage one group can, say, surround another and some interplay may develop between the individuals of one group and those of another. (See illustrations of top juniors in *Creative Dance in the Primary School.*) Or it may be that the two groups continue to dance in their own particular fashion—for example, a stepping group may surround a rising and sinking group.

It is a very big step, however, for one group to preserve an awareness of its own entity and at the same time relate to another. Sometimes this is introduced too soon to pupils or students and all too quickly the class degenerates into the teacher suggesting ideas and producing a development of group interplay. Nevertheless such relationships can be achieved if the class is ready for them. The use of sound—voice, percussion or appropriate music—will sometimes aid this type of group interplay. It is yet another stage of progress when the ideas suggested above can take place without actual touch and this will probably occur more readily with older groups.

From unison action in a group, a further step is that of an action passed through the group as in a rippling movement. In this case the moment of "take-over" asks for sensitivity between members of the group and the constant passage between the individuals needs to be smooth and fluent, to preserve the sense of unity.

In contrast to evolutions in which common shared action is developed, we can explore the possibilities of individual action within a group situation. It is important that this is not left out from the pupils' experience as social situations in real life demand the ability not only to be one of the group in a sympathetic and undisruptive way, but also to take a personal stand if and when necessary.

One way in which this can be introduced is through the use of a common

76

effort rhythm within which individuals use different body parts to lead and to relate to each other. This has already been mentioned in the section in this chapter on effort. Another possibility is the mingling of a group, the members of which have selected their own mode of travelling from an action or an effort or a spatial point of view. There is scope for group awareness if the individuals work out a short personal movement phrase on the same theme—for example, opening and closing with turning or rising and sinking—and then perform this near to several others. Slight adaptations can occur as the individuals become aware of moments of relationship with others in the group. This can spark off a more extensive piece of work on group awareness, especially if the teacher is able to observe the interesting possibilities which are occurring within each group and can draw the pupils' attention to these and so encourage them to develop their ideas further.

Another way in which individual action can lead to group awareness is that of the forming of a group from an individual action or pair action into which the others gradually become involved. For example, an individual or pair may be turning on the spot and other members of the group may be drawn into the flow of the action in turn until this becomes a group movement. In a more spatial context the still position which occurs from the leader binding the flow of action may provide a focus. The rest of the group may then approach in turn and halt their movement flow in a situation which they feel adds to the form established by the leader. A plastic group shape will thus be built up.

There is clearly a point of reference here to three-dimensional work which may be done in art, and those interested in sculpture and three-dimensional constructions will appreciate the common factors. Indeed co-operation with the art department may enable this to be explored at the same time in the two arts. But dance is a dynamic art form and from the plastic group beginning, group motifs will occur. It may be at first that the group can only establish a unity and find ways of dissolving it—parting in unison, in turn, returning by the same route to the first starting-place, or moving through the group to a different place. Eventually, however, the aim is for the *appropriate* group motifs to be discovered and developed. For one group it may be a swaying, for another a stepping pattern, for another an undulating rising and sinking, for another a rotation. The intuitive selection of the possibilities inherent in any particular meeting comes only with practice and with observation of each other's efforts.

Yet another aspect to be explored is the interaction between an individual and a group. Starting as a part of the group action, an individual may suddenly or gradually establish a different movement idea. This may simply be arresting the flow and coming to stillness; it may be separating from the others; it may come about through a change of quality. Whatever form the individual statement takes it may spark off further developments and may lead to integration once more or never achieve the former unity. A different experience is gained if the individual starts apart from the group action. From this starting situation the task is that of finding means to integrate the individual into an existing group motif. The initiative may, of course, come from either the individual or the group. Another possibility is for the individual to draw the others into his or her movement motif and so effect a change in the original group's mood. In the many possibilities of subdivision within the group of five or six, sensitive awareness of others can be called for. For example the interweaving of a line of three within a small circle of three, and a subsequent change whereby the line becomes a circle and the circle a line, would call for sensitivity if such changes were to be carried out smoothly and without halting the flow of the movement.

All these improvisations, explorations and exercises are necessary to form the basis of group dances. "This is an excellent preparation for the performance of dances with group feeling," writes Laban of Theme 14.

CHAPTER 9

Fifth to Seventh Year Secondary, aged 15–18

AT the time of writing year 5 is an "extra" year for many in secondary modern and comprehensive schools but, with the recently announced raising of the school leaving age to 16 in 1973, it will soon become the final year for these pupils. At the same time, for many in comprehensive, grammar and high schools this is the year in which "O" levels are taken. Whether it be on account of G.C.E. or C.S.E., it tends to be a year of academic pressure.

For all pupils, therefore, opportunities to participate in creative work and to take part in group work, rather than emphasise individual powers, are a vital need. For this reason it is not a year in which a lot of new study material should be introduced but the dance lesson should afford the chance for refreshment, practical participation and recreation. The emphasis will be best placed on dance and dance drama compositions, drawing on vocabulary acquired in earlier years. In the selection of themes there should be variety in content and in presentation. From the point of view of content, the stress might be on *action and body awareness*, in which case one might have a dance in which leaping, travelling and turning predominated, or one in which contrasts between simultaneous and successive flow were brought out. The stress might be on *effort*, in which case one might select music of a clear dynamic contrast and group interplay, as for example "Group Dance" by Adda Heynssen. The stress might be on *space*, in which case one might use a three-ring trace form as a basis for the development of a trio.

The result may be in the realm of the lyrical or dramatic, serious or light-hearted, depending upon the choice of material, on the music, if it is used, and upon the harmonious or conflicting relationships developed.

From the point of view of presentation it is important that a variety of methods is used. The teacher may work out the composition in considerable detail, leaving some scope for the pupil's own ideas. For example, the dynamic and spatial content may be set out but the actual relationship in terms of numbers and juxtaposition may be left to the class. The theme may, in contrast to the previous method, be presented in a very broad fashion and the detail worked out by the class. For example, the theme may be that of the changing relationships between three: in unison, and one separating being drawn back, two leaving one and a resolution coming from each trio as they think fit. The dynamics and detailed form and subsequent spatial pattern will be supplied by the trios themselves.

A directed dance study may be taught from time to time or the teacher may be able to work out a choreographed dance.

The use of other starting-points than movement itself may be introduced at this stage, particularly if they are suggested by the pupils themselves. Indeed, ideas for suitable themes should be sought from the classes and worked out with the teacher's help and guidance.

Discretion is needed in planning work from the point of view of selection of material and method. For some classes too much emphasis on the creative side may prove a strain and a balance must be held between this work, which calls for a particular type of participation and involvement, and work in which most of the composition is done by the teacher. In the latter the class share in the invention, giving it life and form through their interpretation of the teacher's ideas.

It may well be that this is the age group, more than any other, for whom music might be used to a considerable degree in order to assist the flow of the dance and in this way serve a special need in enhancing the recreative aspect. While the vast amount of material presented under the heading EFFORT in the previous year will still provide scope for fifth years, where the teacher feels that new material is needed, then additional work may be introduced in the aspects of *Space* and *Relationship* as outlined below.

SPACE—LABAN THEMES II AND I2

Where the pupils have a good grasp of the dimensions, of the planes and of the inclinations which link the planes, as given in detail in the syllabus for years 3 and 4, progress can be made into the exploration of more complex orientation.

In jumps and leaps used in dances the pupils will already be experiencing something of the flying sensation that is associated with movement into the high diagonals.

In exploring the diagonal orientation, a movement sensation of flying towards the high diagonals and falling into the opposite diagonals is gained. Such movement has a labile character and contrasts markedly with the stability of dimensional and plane movements. There is a sense of exhilaration in attempting to use these diagonals with their momentary sense of freedom and asymmetry in the elevation, even when the difficult task of combining three actions is still not mastered fully.

There are endless possibilities of working out simple dance motifs using a diagonal as a basis and discovering the possible transitions along the edges, or across the faces, of the cube to return to the starting-point. Travelling, leaping and turning can all be employed and pair and group plays worked out. There is one proviso to this aspect of the work. It must be within the grasp of the class. Unless, to give only one example, a transition from the high-left-forward diagonal to the high-right-forward one, with right side leading, is seen as an opening, while at the same time, maintaining the rising, advancing character of the action, then an empty mechanical result will occur.

The same must be said of studies devised by the teacher based on the more advanced aspects of space harmony such as the five-rings, A Scale, B Scale or Standard Scale. There is no reason why such pieces of work should not be introduced—if the teacher is thoroughly familiar with the principles underlying their structure and the pupils are able to give expression to the form. Because it will be rare to find pupils who can achieve this, it is not intended to go into this aspect in further detail. Those wishing to become familiar with this aspect should avail themselves of opportunities for further study at courses and can add to their practical studies through a study of *Choreutics*.

RELATIONSHIP—LABAN THEME 15

The material contained in this theme holds a different type of relatedness from that covered in Theme 14. Group formation calls not only for sensitivity in reaction to other members of the group but also for a more abstract spatial awareness. In a line formation a member of the group has to be aware not only of others on both sides of him but also of the shape that the line is making and of his particular part according to his position within the line. The difficulties encountered in participating in a line formation are evident in the example of a line encircling a closely knit group. Only an experienced group will avoid packing closely at the front near the leader and leaving a gap behind the last person.

There is a difference too between a circular formation employed as a suitable starting situation for the experience of group unity, as in contraction and expansion, and the concept of "the circle." In the latter case the individual is aware of the whole structure and, in the example of the circle, his part is to preserve the wholeness of the shared form. The same point can be made in relation to the swaying around the centre of a spiral form which might well have developed from the group travelling in a line formation. Here the spiral shape should be preserved.

Within this theme is contained an understanding, through participation in the various formations, of the particular significance of each one. It is especially important for fifth year pupils to be drawn into discussion on such topics so that they appreciate all that is contained within a movement experience. Indeed, an overall criticism could justifiably be made that insufficient explanation of what lies behind a particular theme takes place. Pupils of this age are interested in comprehending in both an active and an intellectual fashion and there is a need to integrate these methods of learning.

The line holds the possibility of tracing a pathway through the space, of streaming in straight paths, of zigzagging, snaking, curving, twisting and spiralling. It can contract and expand and do this in different parts of the line. It can divide the space of the room into variously shaped areas. Lines can stream past each other, can curve around each other, can interweave. A line can surround a tightly formed group. It can form a barrier. The special characteristic of a line is its long, continuous, winding nature which holds associations with the labyrinth and the maze, thought by some to represent the journey of the dead, and has historical origins with primitive snake dances.

The circle has developed from the idea of encircling, with associations of taking possession of whatever lies within. It reflects the shape of primitive circular and beehive huts. The circle is a complete form concerned with unity and excluding those not a part of the ring. All have an equal part in its movement and there is no leader. The smallest number that can experience anything of a circle is three and it is significant that we think of the firstborn as making the family circle, which may of course increase in size as more children join it.

A block formation in which all face in the same direction has an expression of confrontation. The advancing movements of such a block can convey power, impregnability, solidarity and regimentation. A symmetrically formed block shape suggests conformity and mass response. A block formation which is wedge shaped conveys something different. Here the narrowing to a leader at the front suggests a spearhead of a more offensive and penetrating nature. Because of the forward stress within the group shape this form suggests greater activity than the symmetric block.

Associations in freer group shapes are also possible and here the three-dimensional sculptural possibilities occur. Different levels can be employed and the shapes can be symmetric or asymmetric. The emphasis throughout, however, is on the movement potential and significance of these forms. Formations such as mentioned here may be used in an exploratory fashion or may be used appropriately in dances and dance dramas.

Where sixth-form pupils are having a weekly dance lesson and have had five years' previous experience, advanced themes can be explored with them. Aspects of Themes 11, 12, 14 and 15 will be further explored and used and Theme 16, concerned with the expressive qualities or moods of movements, can be included. As Laban wrote in connection with this theme:

". . . children of the later senior age-group have an urge to explore their own and other people's moods."

The important fact to be conveyed in this theme is that mood in movement derives from the possible combinations of effort qualities. Although words have been given to the compounds which comprise the eight basic effort actions, many other combinations remain unnamed. Perhaps this is just as well as the naming of effort actions has sometimes led into difficulties when discussing their mood, the words having obvious everyday connotations for the non-specialist. Older pupils will be interested in the way in which the use of particular qualities or combinations will produce a characteristic mood. They will be able to appreciate that a change of quality will affect the mood of the movement. In pure dance forms they will use their range of effort to bring about lively, excited, vigorous, delicate or calm moods. In dramatic themes they will be able to penetrate the action to discover the movement moods which will best convey the idea. This calls for an intelligent approach and this is why dramas of strong mood content are best worked out by senior pupils. Perhaps one example will suffice to explain the point. This verse from Isaiah was used as a starting-point:

> "Is not this the fast that I have chosen? to loose the bands of wickedness, to undo the heavy burdens and to let the oppressed go free and that ye break every yoke?"

The first task was to establish motifs which conveyed a situation from which the "loosing," "undoing" and "freeing" could take place. The immediate ideas were those of the first group being held together in a strong grip, the second group stumbling with a sense of heaviness in their bodies and the third group, starting on the ground, pressing upwards as if to remove the oppression. These were merely movement ideas which could form the basis of motifs and be developed with the teacher's help. Finally, the first group created a motif which used a wringing action travelling in a linked formation, the movement of one affecting the movement of another, and from this developed variations and eventually evolved a rondo-form dance phrase. The second group created a stepping motif, the uneven rhythm of which brought them stumbling together into a group which, leaning against each other, sank heavily downwards. The developments in this group lay in alternating the individual's weighty movement with those of the close group. The third group created a rising motif with palms pressing upwards and eventually developed a rhythmical phrase in four parts which they used in canon form.

A good deal of wrestling with the material is needed if the symbolic dance gesture is to be created and the movement is to be given form.

Those who have acquired a deeper knowledge of moods of movement will be familiar with the possibilities of incomplete effort and of the fields of expression contained within the vision, spell and passion drives. These too can be used to deepen and extend the pupils' experience. It is not the scope of this book to elaborate on this aspect in detail. The interested teacher can refer to *Mastery of Movement* where these are elaborated.

The effort content is not the only factor responsible for the mood of movement. Bodily location and the shape of the movement play their part in the total expression. The more subtle possibilities of such combinations provide a vast field of exploration and of material for creative dance expression of interest to sixth formers.

Discussion with those organising the movement experience in the curriculum of the fifth and sixth years shows that in many schools in these years, dance is included as an option along with other physical activities. Another way in which it is made available for older pupils is as a club activity. Where either of these two arrangements is made, as opposed to a regular dance lesson, it is doubtful if much fresh material will be introduced.

The atmosphere generated in the optional class or dance club is one of great enthusiasm and of creative activity and clearly caters for the need of some pupils to balance the academic pressure of their programme. Sometimes the dance club functions as a production group which gives dance performances from time to time. In this case the selection of dance themes suitable for presentation to an audience must be considered carefully. If the dance club puts on a performance, this saves the teacher from making selection for leading parts, and thus appearing to make judgments concerning children's dance ability, as can happen if production work is carried out in class. This is only defensible when the whole class is involved. Best of all is the evening of dance when many classes show the work on which they are currently engaged. Such a demonstration can enable the teacher to introduce the themes being taken with different classes, to point out the variety of response to a given task and thus to build up some idea of the philosophy underlying creative dance.

CHAPTER 10

The teacher's task

It is assumed that the majority of teachers of dance in the secondary school will have received specialist training either in a supplementary dance course, or in a course in movement and dance as a principal or subsidiary subject for study, or as a part of a Physical Education course. This means that, unlike those tackling dance teaching in the primary school, they will have spent a considerable amount of time in becoming familiar with the material included in the preceding chapters on the syllabus and will, in addition, have discussed methods of approach and had the opportunities to try these out during teaching practices. Nevertheless, some points about preparation of material and methods of introducing it may be helpful to student teachers and to those who are consolidating their experience in school.

The theme for the group of lessons will obviously be selected on the basis of the age and experience of the class. The material in the syllabus was laid out according to the aspects of the body, effort, space, relationship appropriate to each stage of development. To the teacher starting the year with a new class two pieces of·advice might be helpful. First, it is wise to select the theme with which the teacher feels most secure personally, and secondly the choice of an aspect of effort with clear bodily activity can often be a sound policy. The concept of effort as the element in movement which is dependent upon inner preparation and full involvement in action demands a concentration which will be helpful to a teacher meeting a class for the first time.

Knowledge of the aspects referred to in the earlier chapters is an essential part of the preparation of the dance teacher. Variety and richness will be brought to the lesson if the teacher has at his finger-tips all the possibilities which may be brought out in relation to a chosen theme. In this way suggestions for enriching or deepening an experience can be given by the teacher. Moreover, this knowledge will enable him to observe the elements which distinguish one child's response to a task from that of another. It is not, of course, only the knowledge of the analysis of movement components that is important. Far more important is an understanding of the correlation in bodily action of the aspects separated only for the purposes of study.

A given theme may be immediately comprehended by an individual or group and given form. In this case the teacher's task is to comment on the way in which the task was fulfilled: to note the use of this or that part of the body, the distinctive effort quality used, the clarity of the trace forms in the space, the awareness of the relationships evolved. In so doing the teacher enhances the individual's or the group's awareness of their achievement and so confirms and strengthens their experience. Another individual or group may be floundering. Here the teacher's task is to observe any glimmer or understanding and work from this. In this case the teacher draws on his knowledge, not so much to observe the achievement, as in the first example, but rather to feed suggestions and ideas and encourage the slightest efforts on the part of the pupils.

In this way the teacher's task is seen as a positive one. The nature of dance, with the requirement of full participation on the part of the class, is such that an approach which is negative or which suggests that the response is "wrong" will be fatal to the establishment of a climate in which creative work can develop.

The structure of the lesson will vary with the experience of the teacher and the level of experience of the class. A simple basic plan for beginners is one in which the class starts with a shared activity, proceeds to personal experience of the chosen material and finally works with others to produce a short dance sequence. The first activity of the lesson serves to bridge the gap between the lessons, usually a week apart; it serves to integrate a class which may be made up of pupils not normally working together, often the case when two classes are put together for dance; it may warm up the group in cold weather. In addition to serving these needs, the beginning of the lesson should cater for more fundamental needs. Thus it should aim to bring the group into the mood for movement and be in the nature of a relaxing and loosening activity. It brings about the relationship between teacher and class which is different from the separateness which often occurs in the classroom where the pupils often sit facing the teacher. In dance the placing of the teacher in the class is of vital importance. To be in the centre of a large circle, to be a part of a circle, to interweave and vary one's position in the room makes for a less formal grouping which is necessary in starting off a lesson.

Finally, the first activity of the lesson should hold the germ of the lesson theme. It is easy for the teacher to build up a series of warming-up activities which are gone through in an automatic fashion and have no bearing on the material to follow. It is, however, possible to use activities which get the class moving without too lengthy a discussion and yet bring them quite quickly into some experience which leads into the lesson theme. When classes have some background they will be able to start off on their own recalling the work of the previous week, where appropriate. This is particularly helpful with more experienced classes who are sustaining a piece of work over several weeks. It can also serve a useful purpose if the theme for the current lesson presents a contrast to that of the week before.

In the basic plan the suggestion was that individual experience of the chosen theme should follow the introductory part of the lesson. Here again it is a question of appropriateness. If the main theme is concerned with relationship then individual work will only be important in serving as a contrast to relationship with others. Indeed it may be a welcome relaxation from the demands of group sensitivity to be given an opportunity to work independently.

Where, however, the material is such that it is possible, there is much to be said for preliminary personal experience. There are several reasons for this. Firstly, it enables the pupil to get to grips with the task for himself. Secondly, it provides scope for his personal response with the consequent varied results from the class as a whole. Thirdly, it means that he is only contending with one problem at a time. In the realm of effort it is almost inevitable that qualities well produced by the individual will deteriorate for a time if a group task using these qualities is given. Only as the problems related to the new situation with others are resolved will the quality improve. When the pupils have more experience, it is possible for them to be given tasks in which the bodily aspects or the effort or the spatial elements are clearly performed at the same time as a relationship is brought about.

We could see this for example in a group task in which individuals use curving pathways to mingle, leading into a travelling in one direction by the whole group. Again, an example might be an approach with a clear body part leading so that all meet for a moment followed by a separation leading with the part furthest from the others. Yet a third example might be the action of thrusting jumps to meet a partner followed by pressing actions in which one causes the other to sink or retreat.

If the introduction to the lesson has led on to the individual work as suggested, then the culmination, and indeed the main part of the lesson, will be pair, trio or group work. This has been discussed in considerable detail in the preceding chapters. The main general point to be made here is that dance provides a rare opportunity for group work which is a shared experience. Because it is now familiar, we do not always emphasise sufficiently either the value of such an experience or the difficulties inherent in it. The value is that of adapting to others: putting forward ideas, listening to others' ideas, working sensitively in spontaneous group inventions and mastering a piece of dance so that one's part in the whole is well integrated; all these are the sort of group interactions which are found in life itself. The difficulties are equally those found in life: some groups can work well together, some individuals find it difficult to become part of a group and always want to take a lead, some individuals are passive and will not take a positive part, some insist on talking when action is the best answer. Clearly the teacher's task is to observe these things and act accordingly. All pupils can be put into the position of leader and led and they can be encouraged to work in different groups. It is all too obvious when an individual is consistently left out of groupings and, apart from attempting to discover the reason, the teacher will have to find ways of integrating this child. It may be to select him as a leader or to choose his movement for a group to follow; it may be to indicate that those sitting near to each other in areas of the room are to form groups and so see that he is included in one of the groups without fuss.

This lesson structure serves simply as a basis. Lessons may start in many ways. After a preliminary warming and loosening up, a group dance may be recalled in its entirety. The lesson may then be used to work at aspects in need of particular attention. A drum rhythm might be played in order to gather together a class as they come into the hall, if the lesson is to be

H 89

based on metrical rhythms. Music which is to form the basis of a dance can be listened to and discussed. Clearly the teacher will not limit himself to one approach only.

In suggesting material for different age groups, the approach suggested here has stressed the importance of developing the "language of movement" as a basis for dance and dance drama. Frequently those new to the work will ask if more "concrete" ideas would be a better choice of material. Two questions emerge: Better for whom? and What is concrete?

The answer to the first question is that a story is often used by the teacher as a substitute for a good grasp of movement vocabulary and it can easily become more important to "get through to the end" than for the children to have a good movement experience. The teacher can also get carried away by seeing the whole story enacted before him and forget about the real aim of the work.

The answer to the second question is that there is surely nothing more tangible than one's own body, nothing more real than bodily action, nothing more able to convey meaning. Ideas, and by that is usually meant stories or poems, can certainly form themes for dance dramas. It is, however, quite erroneous to think that their transmutation into movement is easy. It is very difficult. Dance is concerned with symbolic gesture, not literal description, and the teacher must be able to penetrate deeply into a literary theme in order to discover the movement content. Otherwise the result will be a poor reflection of something conveyed much better in words. If the teacher can do this then there is a wealth of material at his disposal. Contemporary events, myths, stories from the Bible, and particularly poems, will be sources to explore. They must, however, be selected for the movement potential, which the teacher or the pupils find within them. It is for this reason that lists of stories or poems are not provided here. The teacher's and student's own source book is the most valuable aid. A simple test of suitability of material used with students is to ask them to give an account of an idea which they think suitable for dance drama. If their description is full of such phrases as "they thought," "he said," "she had an idea," then the student must be challenged as to the way in which these ideas will be conveyed in action. Even when feelings are mentioned the question of how feelings are to be given expression in movement must be asked.

For the older classes who are concerned with group relationships the ability to use such themes and the wrestling with problems of working them out in a dance form will be a sign of their progress. What is disturbing is the use of long stories with younger age groups so that no time is given to developing a movement vocabulary. Indeed the child's movement experience can be severely hampered as he finds himself, for example, a part of a dragon for several lessons.

When ideas are sought then it is well worth examining poetry as a source. This is because, like dance, poetry is concerned with the essence of an experience, it is frequently full of symbolism, it has a rhythmicality of its own and it frequently explores aspects of a central theme rather than developing a stream of happenings.

To write of using stories and poems as sources of inspiration brings one to the question of integration of subjects in the curriculum. This was discussed in Chapter 2 in connection with possible developments in the middle school. In the secondary school, where there is a high degree of specialisation, the tendency is for few teachers to know what material is being covered with their classes in other subject areas. Sometimes the pupils will provide the bridge by asking if they may dance to a piano piece or record heard in their music lessons. They may also suggest that something encountered in English could be used. In the main, however, any links have to be made by the dance teacher. This can be done by enquiring about topics being taken particularly by older classes or, as suggested in Chapter 3, by older classes to whom dance is being introduced for the first time.

One area in which dance seems to have played an increasingly important part in many schools in the last few years is that of religious education. A number of television religious broadcasts have used dance performed by schoolchildren or students. In the school itself dance is now frequently used as part of the morning services as well as for such special services as those of Christmas time. Dance dramas may be based on such themes as that of the Prodigal, the Good Samaritan, Job, Everyman, Pilgrim's Progress, the Christmas story. Dances of Praise, Thanksgiving and Worship will also have their place. Dance can play a part in this connection since it can help to reveal values and ideas, usually conveyed verbally, in a fresh way. Moreover, the discussion which can take place about the expression and meaning of a particular movement motif can in itself lead to discussion about a significant spiritual idea. When it comes to the need to convey, for example, peace-bringers, the immediate response often suggests a gentle smoothing action. Further reflection will reveal the fact that qualities of sustained effort, of hard work, are needed to bring warring factions together. The blind must be made to look, the deaf have their hands pulled from their ears, the isolated be brought into contact with others. Vague, smoothing actions will not convey this. Discussion about the selection of appropriate actions could throw another light on the nature of peace-making.

Throughout the previous chapters references have been made to the use of sound or music. There are some general points to be made in this connection. Percussion and voice sound can be introduced at any stage once a movement vocabulary has been gained. Percussion can be used as a stimulus to action; it can be added as an accompaniment to action already worked out; it can be used as the movement is worked out, the two going hand in hand. A useful appendix dealing with this aspect is given by Diana Jordan in her book *Childhood and Movement* (Blackwell). First year groups can work to a task with a leader playing an instrument. They can also group together according to the instrument of their choice. Indeed this was one way in which a mixed first year group who preferred to work with either boys or girls together, but never mixed, came to do so. A free choice of instrument was given and the children were then asked to join with others who had selected the same instrument. Thus mixed groups were formed without any difficulty. A variety of instruments can be used for interplay in small groups. With older groups instruments can be introduced as a means of giving a phrase for a group motif and whole percussion dances can be created.

As already indicated a good deal of the first and second year work will be done without piano or recorded music in order to establish the idea of movement having its own inherent rhythm. When music is introduced from time to time use should be made of short pieces and short bands. The "Listen and Move" series have proved successful with first, second and third years. With older groups slightly longer pieces of music can be used. The "Music for Dance" records prepared principally for use with the motif-writing books have been used for dances. It is not the intention here to give lists of music for different age groups. Finding suitable music for themes is a part of the lesson preparation and it is only in tackling a listening programme and keeping notes of music heard on radio, television and at concerts that the teacher can become knowledgeable. Every experienced dance teacher will know that many hours have to be spent in finding music, and frequently listening to much which is not immediately useful, but, in this way, a knowledge of the style of different composers is gradually acquired so that the task becomes less exacting over the years.

The main problem is in selecting music for a particular theme. To use music by too many composers in one dance will destroy artistic unity and the idea often has to be modified in order to preserve this unity. Ideally of course suitable music composed for the dance is really required. Only rarely is such an accompanist found.

For all pupils, whether of primary or secondary age, the dance lesson should provide opportunities for exploration, for mastery and for creativity. Exploration is called for when new material is presented as a challenge; when, for example, a class is asked to discover the possibilities of interaction in a group of five, or when, to give another example, the pupils are discovering with which parts of the body they can successfully perform a phrase of thrust–slash–flick. Exploration may be in the form of improvisation on a particular theme, an invaluable way of discovering new possibilities in movement since the emphasis is on spontaneous action rather than a carefully reasoned movement idea.

Mastery is constantly called for as the pupils are asked to clarify their dance phrases. This calls for self-discipline so that the movement is not woolly and meaningless. Clarity in the body, in the effort exerted, in the spatial form and in relationship are all to be looked for. The more experienced the class, the more can be expected in this respect. This is another sign of progress in the work. Mastery may be asked for in clarification of the pupils' own inventions or it may involve working on the dance motif invented by another pupil or invented by the teacher. This second process takes even more time than the first, since mastering another's motifs can be difficult and time-consuming if the performance is not to be a faltering copy. There is a place for such experience since it may serve to extend the individual's personal range. The danger lies of course in the selection of

93

the motifs. They must be within the grasp of the class and they must be well taught so that the expression of the movement is clearly understood and conveyed.

The process involved in learning the movements devised by others implies that the pupil has a preconceived model to which he does his best to conform. This is quite different from the experience of engaging in creative activity where the final result is not envisaged.

Creativity is a concept that raises many questions. First of all it seems to be difficult to analyse, although it is recognisable. Secondly, we have to consider why it should be rated so highly. Thirdly, we have to try to discover the conditions which render it possible for children to work creatively. A number of writers have been interested in penetrating this aspect of human endeavour. One approach is to examine the verbal statements of people generally agreed to be creative artists. This was done in the collection of writings *The Creative Process*. In *Creativity in the Arts* the papers of a number of distinguished artists and philosophers are brought together in order to clarify ideas about this topic.

When we speak of creative dance in a school situation we have to see creativity in a different light from that of the creative artist who produces original works of art. Some elements in the process are, however, present in the school situation. Although in dance lessons we are not expecting great works of genius we do look for something original from that child or group of children. It is important that we do not over-value novelty. The once fashionable question "in how many ways" can the task be answered is suspect for its lack of judgment and selection. Appropriateness is more significant than novelty. We see in a piece of creative work more than self-expression. The child can express himself in a stamp or a shrug or a jump but this is no work of artistic merit. The self-expression must communicate what it intends to communicate and must be recognised by the performer as doing so. This is what we mean when we say that a movement "speaks." The inner state has been manifest in expression which has a form consciously perceived.

We rate creative activity highly because of its personal nature. Putting our own mark on an activity, saying something our own way, making something of our own are signs of our need to express our individuality in

94

concrete form. The ability to achieve independent works brings personal satisfaction and confidence. Moreover, we know and can recall more readily things which we have created for ourselves. Since we consider creative activity of value to the child and adolescent in helping him to find his personal powers of expression in different fields, we have to consider how the atmosphere can be established for this process to take place. The creative artist who composes, writes, dances, paints will do this at the time most appropriate to his temperament. In school we have a time set apart for a subject and, while this may not be absolutely true of primary schools, it is an almost universal picture of secondary schools. For this reason the dances created may only rarely fall into the true category of works of art.

Most writers on the topic of creativity agree that there are certain stages in the creative process. Problems are presented and thrust themselves forward for solution; material has to be consciously manipulated; time is needed for the idea to grow, to be mulled over, to be dreamt about; there may be moments of inspiration. In the dance lesson the teacher has the task of thrusting the problem in front of the pupils. It may appeal to some and not to others. Rarely is the time sufficient for the growth and the dreaming. Indeed this process is usually experienced more by the teacher in developing themes for lessons or dances. Some may suggest themselves in a flash and remain unused for years until the right moment occurs. Of the other stages, moments of inspiration may and do occur and the material is certainly consciously manipulated. Different solutions may be tried; different combinations may be made; the dance motifs, the variations, the developments, the contrasting moods will be established and clarified.

To those interested in creativity the books of Jerome K. Bruner, *The Process of Education* and *On Knowing—essays for the left hand,* prove most thought-provoking. This is particularly so because Dr. Bruner, Professor of Psychology at Harvard, is concerned to examine the nature of teaching and learning. In the second of the books mentioned above he suggests that a working definition of creativity is that it is an act that produces effective surprise. He writes:

"I would propose that all the forms of effective surprise grow out of combinational activity—a placing of things in new perspectives."

95

In discussing the conditions of creativity he sets out a number of para-doxes. Of "detachment and commitment" he says:

"But it is a detachment of commitment. For there is about it a caring, a deep need to understand something, to master a technique, to render a meaning."

Of "passion and decorum" he says:

"By passion I understand a willingness and ability to let one's impulses express themselves in one's life through one's work.

. . . But again a paradox: it is not all urgent vitality. There is a decorum in creative ability: a love of form, an etiquette towards the object of our efforts, a respect for materials."

Of freedom to be dominated by the object he writes:

"As the object takes over and demands to be completed 'in its own terms,' there is a new opportunity to express a style and an individuality."

Bruner highlights conditions of creativity, which one would suggest the teacher of dance must have in mind, for they are of great significance. The teacher's role is a creative one too. He must care deeply about the children's creative attempts and so encourage them to do likewise. He and they must be able to stand back and to master techniques and render meanings. Vitality and passionate involvement are needed as is the love of form. The need to let the work of art "take over" is of vital importance so that a piece of work has its own integrity and unity and is not merely a contrivance.

All this demands of the teacher the power to stimulate and interest a class in a theme. It demands observation so that the pupils are helped to select and formulate the material for their dances. It asks for sensitive participation in choosing the time to make helpful comments and in knowing when to stand apart. Most of all it demands from the teacher the ability to gain satisfaction from the children's creative endeavour. It is easy to fall into the trap of satisfying oneself in teaching a set pattern to a class or in using the class as raw material for the interpretation of one's own creative aspirations in dance.

The dance teacher needs to keep alive his own creative ability through participating in recreative dance groups, movement choirs and vacation courses or in taking part in dance productions. In this way he will not only fulfil his own needs but will appreciate the needs of the children he teaches. Through creative dance experience the inner feelings are given expression and are formulated in a symbolic and universal language which communicates to others. To quote Bruner again:

"Sharing then, and the containment of impulse in beauty—these are the possibilities offered by externalisation."

A Selected Bibliography of books quoted or referred to in the text

Bruner, J. K.	*On Knowing.*	Harvard University Press	(1962).	Pp. 20, 23–26 and 32.
Ghiselin, B. (Ed.)	*The Creative Process.*	Mentor	(1952).	
Jordan, D.	*Childhood and Movement.*	Blackwell	(1966).	Appendix 2.
Laban, R.	*Modern Educational Dance.*	Macdonald & Evans	(1963).	Pp. 12, 33, 41, 48 and 50.
Laban, R.	*Mastery of Movement.*	Macdonald & Evans	(1960).	Pp. 84–85 and 92.
Laban, R. and Ullmann, L.	*Choreutics.*	Macdonald & Evans	(1967).	
Meerloo, J. A. M.	*The Dance.*	Chilton Book Co.	(1960).	P. 42.
Muschenheim, W.	*Elements in the Art of Architecture.*	Thames & Hudson	(1965).	P. 13.
Munro, T.	*The Creative Arts in American Education.*	Harvard University Press	(1960).	P. 5.
Noverre Trans. Beaumont, C. W.	*Letters on Dancing and Ballet.*	Dance Horizons	(1966).	P. 38.
Preston-Dunlop, Valerie	*Handbook for Modern Educational Dance.*	Macdonald & Evans	(1963).	
Semeonoff, B. (Ed.)	*Personality Assessment.*	Penguin Books	(1966).	Chapter 2.
Shawn, T.	*Every Little Movement.*	Eagle Printing and Binding Company	(1954).	P. 25.
Sitwell, E.	*Taken Care Of.*	Hutchinson Publishing Co. Ltd.	(1966).	Pp. 43–124.
Thomas, Vincent (Ed.)	*Creativity in the Arts.*	Prentice-Hall	(1964).	

Music referred to in the text

The *Listen and Move* Series (Green Label). Records 3, 4, 5, 6, 7 and 8.
The *Listen and Move Music Books* (1 and 2).
The *Modern Dance* Series (Red Label). Records 1, 2, 3 and 4.
A Pageant of Dances (Blue Label). Records 1 and 2.
Music for Dance (Orange Label). Series A: Records 1, 2 and 3.
　　　　　　　　　　　　　Series B: Records 1 and 2.

Index

Accompaniment, 13, 51, 68, 92
Allport, 15–16, 17
Architecture, 27
Art of movement, 12, 17, 28
Arts, the, 12, 77, 94
Asymmetry, 22, 35–36, 58, 81

Basic effort actions, 38, 56–57
Basic movement themes, 45–46
Body activities, 28, 33–35, 39, 48, 49–52
    awareness, 28, 48–50, 55, 61, 70–71
    flow, 28, 36
    parts, 28, 35, 41, 49, 56, 61, 70, 71, 87
    shape, 22, 48, 55, 58
        arrow, 36, 58
        ball, 37, 58
        screw, 37, 58
        wall, 37, 58
Bound flow, 38, 50
Bruner, J. S., 95, 96, 97

Creativity, 12, 21, 80, 87, 93–97
Cutforth, R., 16

Dance composition, 57, 68, 79–80
    forms, 68, 70, 84, 91
Dance, spring corn, 14–15
Delsarte, 17
Diagonals, 40, 71, 73, 81
Dimensions, 25, 72, 73, 81
Directness, 37, 50, 51, 71
Door plane, 39, 64–65, 73
Drama, 27, 29, 30, 31, 55, 64, 69, 79

Effort, 28–29, 37, 50–52, 55–57, 61–64, 71–72
    qualities, 29, 37, 38, 55, 69, 83, 87
    transitions, 29, 55, 61–64, 71
Elevation, 34, 61, 63, 71
Exploration, 25, 28, 29, 53, 54, 78, 80, 83, 85, 93

Fine touch, 37, 50, 51, 52, 71
Firmness, 37, 50, 51, 52, 71
Flexibility, 37, 50, 52, 71

Form, 22, 27, 58, 59, 66, 68, 72, 80, 82
Free flow, 38, 50

Gesture, 17, 22, 27, 29, 31, 34, 35, 49, 52, 57, 61–64
Group action, 75
    feeling, 58, 70, 74–78
    formations, 31, 81–83
    interplay, 63, 71, 76
    relationships, 51, 66–69, 70, 91
    rhythms, 29, 63
    situations, 22, 31, 89

Improvisation, 53, 54, 59, 66, 68, 78, 93
Inclinations, 73–74
Integration, 12, 21–22, 31, 91

Juniors, 19, 24, 76

Kinaesthetic sense, 54
Kinesphere, 73

Laban, R., 11, 15, 17, 21, 31, 45, 57, 61, 69, 78, 83
Levels, 29–30, 38–39, 52, 59
Locomotion, 33, 48, 49, 65, 74

Masters, J., 14–15
Moods, 16–17, 44, 54, 55, 56, 66, 70, 75, 78, 83–85, 87
Motifs, 31, 63, 64, 66–69, 73–74, 77–78, 81, 84, 93–94
Movement characteristics of age groups, 19, 44, 48, 54, 60, 70, 79–80
Munro, T., 12
Music, 22, 27, 32, 53, 64, 70, 76, 79, 90, 92, 93, 99

Noverre, 16–17

Orientation, 39, 54, 64, 72–74, 80

Pairs, 22, 30, 53, 58, 66, 73, 74, 89
Pattern, air, 29, 39, 40–41, 49–52, 57–58, 72
    floor, 28, 41, 49–52, 58, 64, 72, 82

Percussion, 51, 53, 63, 68, 76, 92
Planes, 39–40, 64–66, 72, 81
Poetry, 22, 26, 31, 90, 91
Posture, 17, 27, 31, 44
Primary school, 12, 59, 86

Relationship, 22, 30–31, 33, 41, 52–53, 58–59,
    63, 65, 66–69, 74–78, 81–83
Religious education, 91–92
Rhythm, 16, 17–18, 21, 26, 27, 29, 53, 55, 61–64,
    71, 77

Sculpture, 18, 77
Sitwell, E., 26
Space, 29–30, 33, 52, 57–58, 64–66, 72–74, 80–81
    harmony, 74, 81

Spatial actions, 25, 29–30, 34–35, 39, 54, 81
Spontaneity, 12, 48, 53, 68, 89, 93
Suddenness, 37, 50, 51, 52, 71
Sustainment, 37, 50, 51, 52, 71
Symbolism, 31, 66, 84, 90, 91, 97
Symmetry, 12, 35–36, 54, 73, 75, 83

Table plane, 39, 65, 68, 73
Trace forms, 74, 79, 87
Trios, 22, 30, 53, 58–59, 66, 74, 79–80, 89

Visual arts, 13, 18, 22, 27

Wheel plane, 39–40, 65, 68, 73